# A DESIGNER'S GUIDE TO INTERVIEWING

## TANNER CHRISTENSEN

# CONTENTS

# INTRODUCTION

*"This isn't going to work. Come back in a year or two when you've had a chance to gain a bit more relevant experience."*

The recruiter saying this had just pulled me out of the first hour of what was supposed to be an intensive, five-hour batch of interviews at the headquarters of a San Francisco tech company.

It was evident I wasn't a good fit for the role of designer at the company however—as I stumbled through imaginary product ideas in front of a whiteboard, everyone seemed to know it. My day-long trip to San Francisco on the company's dime ended with the recruiter walking me to the office front door to tell me the interview would not continue and that the day was mine to do with it whatever I want. I vividly remember her telling me I should enjoy the remainder of the day by exploring the city.

That afternoon I did explore San Francisco, but rather than taking in the city's sights, I walked along the bay waters with my head down, mulling over what I could have done better in the interview. I couldn't think about anything more than what felt like a complete failure. I felt as though I had lost my chance to land the type of job I had dreamed of reaching for a decade: working as a digital designer for an esteemed tech company in the heart of Silicon Valley. What made the company so unimpressed they dismissed me before I had a chance to warm up in the interview, I wasn't sure. Why does anyone fail an interview in the first place? Is "fail" even the appropriate word to use when an interview ends with rejection? If not "failure," then what?

In the years since that frustrating and disappointing interview, I have spent considerable time thinking and talking with others about the process designers go through to get a job. I've learned a lot and, as a result, successfully received job offers from more than two dozen notable companies including Google, Redfin, Uber, Cruise, Atlassian, and Meta (previously Facebook, where I worked for nearly four years). I've also been a design hiring manager at a three-year-old recruiting software company once valued at $1.2 billion. It was there, at the software startup, that I learned even more about the world of recruiting and the processes many companies use to find, assess, nurture, and hire designers.

Over the past ten years of my career, I've seen the ins and outs of recruiting and interviewing as a designer for some of the world's most competitive positions. I've had an opportunity to mingle with some of the top recruiting and design leaders at companies like Apple, Netflix, Amazon, Salesforce, Capital One, Intuit, Deloitte, HubSpot, Adobe, and many more. Through these experiences and conversations, I've learned much about what makes interviewing challenging and rewarding—for job candidates and companies. I have shared what I've learned primarily in private conversations or the occasional social media post, but have never consolidated the insights I've gleaned into a central place for others—until now.

What follows in the pages of this guide are the years of experience I have had in addition to the insights and lessons I've picked up from others; some of whom are far more experienced in interviewing and hiring than I have been. I've compiled these pages of perspective and insights after hearing from many hundreds of designers who struggle consistently to navigate the challenging and often daunting interviewing process. While I have written many insights shared throughout this guide with digital product designers in mind—

designers adept at working on software product strategy, interaction design, and visual design—the lessons apply to designers of all industries and expertise.

I designed this guide with one overarching goal: to help designers like you learn how to interview better. If you put down this book someday soon and feel more confident in your ability to communicate with interviewers, or with a more defined career path, or a clear idea of how to shine in your next interview, I will have accomplished my goal.

But—as with any self-managed endeavor—this guide will only benefit you as much as you're willing to invest in the information provided. The guide offers an incredible amount, and it can be a lot to take in at once. To get the most, you should be clear about what you want to achieve and find ways to incorporate what you uncover.

## HOW TO GET THE MOST FROM THIS GUIDE

If you're curious about what this guide offers before you dig in, explore the table of contents and freely jump between various chapters or sub-sections to get a feel for what's offered. But to get the most value from the guide, it would be best if you define a goal (or set of goals) you want to achieve by reading this guide. Some example goals that might inspire you are:

- Learn what recruiters look for in early conversations so I can better convey my strengths on phone calls.
- Build a more compelling set of interviewing collateral to share with teams and get my dream job.
- Figure out what I could do better in final stage interviews to get job offers.
- Learn what hiring managers look for in junior design portfolios and how I can build one that works for me.

Once you have a goal in-mind for what you want from this guide, I strongly encourage you to write it down somewhere. If you feel comfortable: write your goal down in a place where others can see and hold you accountable to it (such as social media). Then revisit what you've written down at the end of each chapter to ensure you're still aligned and focused on what you hope to get by investing time in reading through the guide.

If you still need to figure out what a goal looks like for you, jump to the chapter section on identifying career goals (chapter 2), then come back here to learn more about getting value from this guide after you've determined a goal or two for yourself.

In addition to setting a goal, it's essential to incorporate what you read into your daily life and engage with others about what you learn. If you read something that stands out to you—either because you are surprised by it, disagree with it, or are curious to know more—consider posting a quote from the book on social media and asking for others' thoughts and experiences on the subject.

I want nothing more for you than to be rewarded in your design career by not taking every piece of information in this book as gospel or for granted. To do that, you will need to not only reflect on what you uncover, but find opportunities to discuss it with others. Research has consistently shown that when someone takes something they learn and shares it, they're more likely to remember it and get a more accurate picture of what it conveys. The only way to ensure that is by inviting you to openly and repeatedly share and invoke conversation from what you read on these pages.

I am thrilled you and thousands of designers like you have leaped to learn about design recruiting and interviewing. I sincerely hope you learn much from what follows. Yet, the value you get from this guide is ultimately up to you. The more time you spend *doing something* with what you uncover, the more likely you will get in return. I've provided some keys, but only you can turn them and open the door.

# ONE
# UNDERSTANDING RECRUITING

## 1. THE RECRUITING PROCESS

What better place to start a pursuit of understanding than at the heart of any job search: recruiting. Recruitment is a complicated process that takes a lot of time and energy, and recruiting strategies are often just as complex as design ones.

If you've ever gone through an interview process with a company only to find they were slow to schedule conversations or delayed in letting you know what they were doing to help you move through the process, this won't come as a surprise. Recruiting is an entirely human-to-human process, so navigating things like priorities, goals, ambitions, and even emotions, can be tricky. Such processes often require a delicate and personal touch, but also an ability for recruiters to manage dozens or hundreds of job candidates at a single time.

The traditional recruitment process typically involves advertising a position, interviewing candidates, and negotiating salaries. Many new applications and tools are coming out to help streamline the process, making it more efficient and effective for companies and applicants, however, human-to-human interaction is still the way every company operates when it comes to hiring.

Despite common myths of automated recruiting software rejecting candidates, there are no companies today that entirely rely on automated software to find, analyze, and hire designers. At most, software today helps automate communication with job candidates and highlighting specific keywords in a résumé, but that's about it. When you look at the amount of work any typical recruiting team goes through, you'll see that automation can only really help them in a handful of ways.

For any job, there are typically six recruiting stages:

1. Planning and alignment
2. Inbound and outbound sourcing
3. Screening and early-stage interviewing
4. Selecting and late-stage interviewing
5. Hiring
6. Onboarding

We won't go into too much detail on each stage here. But to understand why a recruiter or hiring manager is reaching out to you or asking specific questions, it can be helpful to understand a little about each stage of their process as it relates to your experience with them.

**1. Planning and alignment**

The first step to any job creation is determining business needs. In some businesses, headcount planning takes place on a regular or semi-regular cadence. This planning process involves evaluating available business financials, upcoming production needs, and more. Often a specific budget is allocated to a team, and it's up to the unit head or hiring manager to determine what level of hire is needed and within what amount of available budget.

Designer salaries and compensation are not typically allocated up-front. Instead, they are determined later in the recruiting process as hiring gets underway, and the team can better predict what they'll need to spend on their budget. Though teams built on rigid planning may be given a total budget to utilize on an annual basis, and it's up to the team leaders to determine if they want to spend all of the budget on a single, high-level hire, or several less-experienced hires. These decisions are determined by evaluating the business needs—including financial goals and team makeup—above all else.

Once there's enough clear need for a role, a recruiter (or team of recruiters) is assigned the position. They work with the hiring manager, design team, and others to define the job, responsibilities, and ideal persona. The recruiter will describe each job in terms of required skills, knowledge, experience, amount of work available, geographic location, and any special requirements such as spoken languages or additional certifications.

## 2. Inbound and outbound souring

Companies find designers through two primary processes: inbound and outbound sourcing. (Though it is worth noting that referrals—where someone already at the company recommends someone else they are close with outside for a job—is one of the most successful ways to find and land a job.)

Inbound sourcing is when a designer applies to a job through the company website or a job board like LinkedIn, Authentic Jobs, Dribbble, or Indeed. However, many companies also actively engage in outbound sourcing, a process of searching for, connecting with, and building relationships with designers in hopes of transitioning them into job candidates.

Inbound sourcing means a recruiter or hiring manager (or both) will review resumes through their Applicant Tracking System, or ATS. Most common ATSes like Greenhouse and Lever can help expedite the review process by automatically highlighting relevant skills or details in resumes for recruiters. Though automation is additive to inbound recruiting flows, there is no software yet today that automatically rejects or approves a resume for interviewing.

To build outbound sourcing, a company might hire an expert (known as a "sourcer") or an external company such as a staffing agency to find, interact with, and interview designers, and introduce them to the company. Sometimes outbound sourcing is accomplished through presentations at industry conferences or in-person events such as university recruiting events, or "cold outreach" through websites like LinkedIn, Dribbble, or Twitter.

The issue is that it can be difficult for recruiters to find the perfect match for their needs with so many possible candidates and often somewhat vague business requirements. Additionally, not every designer is looking for a new job or a job in a specific industry or locale. To match the right person with the proper position, recruiters and their teams will cast a wide net to catch the attention of someone who is an optimal candidate. At that point, the next step of the recruiting process begins.

**3. Screening and early-stage interviews**

Once a designer has shown interest in an opportunity, the recruiter's job is to talk to them and conduct additional "screening." This part of the recruiting process comes down to assessing the designer on attributes such as minimum skill requirements, career ambitions, expectations, timelines, and cultural alignment.

A recruiter's job is to find the best candidate for the open job. They are looking for someone who will fit the company culture and values well, and who can do the job at-hand. The recruiter will work with you to find out your strengths, weaknesses, and what you're looking for in a new job. They want to know if you can solve problems, navigate complex situations, work well with others, and if you have any questions about the job.

Early stage interviews are critical because they're one of the few chances that a recruiter and hiring team have to get to know you as a person, not just as an applicant. It's also one of their only ways of finding out if they think you would be a good fit for the company. As a designer, you should approach early conversations with recruiters the same way: you won't know for sure whether an opportunity is one worth considering or not until you talk a bit with the recruiter. Being open-minded and honest in conversations with recruiters usually only benefits you (and them).

The first few interviews can take several formats depending on the company's recruiting process. Most typically, you'll see discussions early-on in interviewing like these:

- **Recruiter phone call.** A one-on-one call with a recruiter to discuss the overarching job opportunity and fit.
- **Hiring manager phone call.** A video or phone call with the hiring manager to further assess things like skills-to-job-description match and designer ambitions.
- **Virtual design critique.** A 30 to 45-minute video or phone call to review some design, typically a popular product or website. Hiring teams design these calls to assess what types of things you look at when reviewing strategies in the real world.
- **Discussing past work.** Another 30 to 45-minute call wherein you can talk about one or two projects from the past. Ideally, these calls require no preparation and should be considered a friendly conversation about your experience working on projects.
- **At-home design exercise.** Sometimes, a company may ask you to do an "at-home" exercise, like designing something from scratch such as a dog walking app or ecommerce website.

Note: I personally do not advocate for at-home design exercises because they require uncompensated time from the designer and can limit their ability to take on other projects or work. Such assignments are largely unfair and create inequitable situations. However, some companies need these exercises as a part of the interview process to properly evaluate a candidate's abilities, so they continue offering them. In a later chapter we'll discuss how to navigate these assignments and even decline them respectfully if you feel so inclined.

It should be a personal decision to participate in any at-home design exercise or not. In general, it can be fun to do the training and allow you to demonstrate your skills. However, if the company asks you to redesign something of theirs, it's a red flag. You should never be asked to participate in a biased and possible unpaid working situation while pursuing a job. In such circumstances, you may request a more neutral exercise prompt or compensation for the work.

### 4. Selecting and late-stage interviews

After initial conversations and interviews, the company and you as a design candidate should feel pretty good about the opportunity and "fit." What remains for you and the company to see is if early assessments are accurate. If you're still unsure about taking on the job at this point, ask yourself if you have enough information to determine whether it's an opportunity worth continuing to explore or not.

At this stage of the recruiting process, recruiters and their teams will be looking to evaluate whether early assessments of skills and abilities are accurate. To do that, companies will engage in late-stage interviews such as:

- **Portfolio presentation.** The portfolio presentation is often done as a slideshow and should be when you emphasize your journey with one or two projects. A 45-minute to one-hour presentation recruiting teams hope to be a more informal way to show your work.
- **Problem-solving interviews.** Problem-solving—or design challenges—are small exercises wherein an interviewer or two will ask you to solve a hypothetical problem in real-time. Something like "how would you design a new website for a clothing company? "Design challenges are a highly effective way to signal skills that aren't always evident in a portfolio, like a problem-solving strategy, product thinking and scope analysis, communication, collaboration, prioritization, and so on.
- **Culture or values interviews.** In some companies, an interviewer will ask questions to assess your working values. That is: what are your principles when working with others? It's ok if you don't have any personal values defined, simply speaking to recurring habits and behaviors is what interviewers are trying to assess.

## 5. Hiring

The last stage of the recruiting process includes discussing and negotiating compensation, determining the start date, and providing you with a vocal and then tangible offer.

Some companies will have a set salary range for the position they are hiring for. They will use this to determine what salary to offer you based on the skills and abilities you conveyed during the interview process. It's important to note that good companies will use industry data from research companies like Radford to create equitable and fair compensation for various roles and levels of experience. However, you can still negotiate base salary compensation, ask for a signing bonus (anywhere from 5-12% of the annual base salary) and equity if the company offers some form of stock units or shares to employees.

## 6. Finally, onboarding.

Designers may think signing a new job offer is the end of the recruiting process, but a recruiter's job isn't done until your first day of work—internally, recruiters refer to it as "butt in seat." To help you get to that point, recruiters and hiring managers will help you get basic information about the company culture, benefits, and policies and introduce you to other team members.

## 2. WHO YOU'LL MEET DURING INTERVIEWING

Knowing who you'll meet before an interview can enable you to understand their role and responsibilities. If you can understand what an interviewer will be working on learning from you, you'll be able to maximize every conversation.

On the flip side, if you don't know with whom you'll be speaking, it can be difficult to answer their questions in a manner that delivers confidence and alignment. Learning each interviewer's role and responsibility allows you to manage expectations and get the most from every interaction. The easiest and most reliable way to learn about an interviewer is to ask the recruiter or coordinator to share more information about whoever you'll be speaking to. You can also look up interviewers on social networks like LinkedIn, however, that will only get you a preview of their tailored profile and not much detail into what they will be speaking to you about.

A standard design recruiting team includes not only a recruiter and hiring manager but also a sourcer, recruiter, design interview panel, and more. Throughout interviewing, you will talk to many people across these different roles. Each person you speak with will strive to learn about you while minimizing bias through an objective interview process.

Here I'll share a few of the most common roles you'll likely encounter when interviewing. I share these roles so that you can anticipate better where you are in the interview process and what precisely each person may want to focus on during each conversation.

### Sourcers

Sourced job candidates—those companies find and reach out to first—are 4-5 times more likely to be hired for a job than candidates who apply to a position on a job board or company website (according to a 2022 study by Gem.com, the recruiting software company I previously served as Head of Design at).

Not every company uses full-time sourcers, but those who do find that having a dedicated person to find and connect with designers early-on is an excellent way to cast a wide net and find ideal candidates. A sourcer spends their day planning, prioritizing, and engaging in outreach to designers. When you get a message or email from a company saying they looked at your profile and want to talk to you, it's likely because a sourcer trained to identify promising candidates found your resume or portfolio and liked it enough to reach out.

As a job candidate, you won't always interact with a sourcer. Sometimes, they will connect to you on behalf of someone else on the team, like a recruiter or hiring manager. In such situations the person on the other end of the email could either be a recruiter, hiring manager, or a leader at the company. You won't really know until you start engaging with them to learn more about the opportunity.

### Recruiters

The craft of a recruiter is in managing the complex crossroads of people and business needs: identifying capable designers who can not only support the business but who the business can support as well.

However, because they're not designers does not mean recruiters aren't often exceptionally skilled at understanding the nuances of what makes design work impactful. The best recruiters spend time aligning with design leaders in their organization and staying on top of evolving design trends to understand what makes design meaningful in a business.

When possible, be open and honest with recruiters about your expectations and feelings throughout the recruiting process. If they can do something to make things go better for you, they will. And because their managers evaluate recruiters on their ability to find and hire designers, they are often inclined to see you succeed in the interview process.

Recruiters are some of the best allies and advocates you can have throughout the interviewing process.

### Recruiting coordinator

A recruiting coordinator schedules interviews and calls for the team. Their role is to work with you and others on the recruiting team to accommodate your schedule and needs. The recruiting coordinator will often work behind the scenes to schedule interviews, coordinate recruiting plans and expectations with everyone, and reschedule conversations as needed.

Yet, because they have such an intimate connection to everyone else in the interview process, I always encourage designers to spend time asking coordinators a question or two whenever you can. Getting the coordinator's perspective on the company, their recruiting process, and what makes the coordinator excited to work at the company, can often signal the authentic culture of the business more than you can get elsewhere.

Sourcers, recruiters, and coordinators function at the beginning, or top, of the recruiting funnel. Meaning they sometimes work with hundreds of designers at once. Be mindful that if a recruiter doesn't follow up with you immediately, it's likely not because they don't value you or because you bombed a conversation, but instead, they may be dealing with other priorities.

**Hiring manager**

A hiring manager is the primary person responsible for filling the job. They're often a Design Manager, Director of Design, or someone in a similar people management role. You may or may not get a chance to speak with the hiring manager while interviewing, depending on company size, but if you can: ask to speak with them and get to know their expectations for the role.

There is no other person at a company who better understands the needs that are being hired for than the hiring manager. They will be uniquely qualified to talk about the opportunity, challenges, and ideal candidate for the job.

The hiring manager has the final say on whether to hire a person or not, but they leverage feedback from everyone on the "hiring committee," including the recruiter. In most cases (though not always), the hiring manager is also the person you, as a job candidate, will work directly with if hired. So it's a good idea to get to know them and their expectations as much as possible throughout the interview process.

## Peer designers

In addition to talking to a recruiter and hiring manager, you may have a chance to interview peer designers on the team. The job of a peer designer during an interview is commonly to assess specific design skills such as visual design and craft, interaction design, strategic thinking, communication, collaboration, or self-awareness.

Because they're designers themselves, peer design interviews are specifically to talk shop: what are your strengths and areas for improvement when it comes to designing? What will you be able to add to the existing team? Can you see yourselves working together? How do you talk about your past experiences?

## Cross-functional peers

Lastly, optimal recruiting processes will include a late-stage interview with one or more cross-functional peers at the company: writers, engineers, marketing managers, sales managers, and so on. These peers will often be someone on the marketing, product, sales, or engineering teams, and it's their job to evaluate soft skills. How do you communicate with people who are not design-savvy? How do you convey your work values? What would it mean to work as a partner with you?

While no two teams may be the same in their makeup, the best recruiting practices enable design candidates to talk with many different people in the company. When you are able to speak to various functional members in a company, you can create a more realistic and diverse perspective of the company.

Please take advantage of each conversation by talking about the other person's expectations and responsibilities related to their role in the recruiting process. Doing so will not only enable you to better connect with the person interviewing you, but also give you the information you need to turn the interview into an effective conversation.

## 3. HOW DESIGN RECRUITING TEAMS OPERATE

In today's world, the recruiting process has changed dramatically from what it was just a decade ago. Companies are no longer relying on old-fashioned advertising on websites or hiring headhunters to find the best designers. Instead, companies use modern technology and data-driven approaches to identify, attract and hire designers wherever they are.

Today, recruiting teams include not only recruiters but also sourcers, coordinators, and other specialists. These individuals work across functional teams (not only design but also engineering, marketing, sales, product, etc.) to align on business needs and connect with talented designers. No two recruiting teams will operate identically, but most modern recruiting teams align with most of the following points:

**They use data to inform their decisions.**

Recruiting teams today are using data to inform every decision they make. They track data points such as number of designers messaged, time-to-fill a role, quality of hire (based on time in a role), and cost-per-hire, to help them understand what's working and what's not in their recruiting process.

Using quantifiable data allows recruiters to optimize their approach to get the best results. So when a recruiter reaches out to you with what seems like a spammy message, be mindful that their internal data may indicate outbound messages are much more likely to get attention than other methods. You can help recruiters by replying to messages even when you're not interested in the job. Saying "No thanks" is a certifiable way to ensure the recruiter doesn't message you for that particular role again, while also giving the company data on what messaging works and what messaging is ineffective.

**They use technology to automate repetitive tasks.**

Many repetitive tasks are involved in recruiting, such as posting jobs, screening resumes for specific qualifications, and scheduling interviews. Recruiting teams today are using technology to automate these tasks to focus on more strategic work, such as understanding someone's skills, ambitions, and alignment with company needs through face-to-face conversation.

Most recruiting teams use an applicant tracking system (or ATS). This system allows them to track the many applications they receive and helps them identify the most qualified candidates. The ATS may also conduct initial screening interviews and schedule follow-up interviews with the most promising candidates.

**They use social media to reach candidates.**

Social media is a powerful tool for recruiting because it's where many of us are active online. Messaging people through social media such as Twitter, LinkedIn, Slack, TikTok, etc., allows recruiters to reach many candidates quickly and easily. It might sound impersonal, but more and more younger generations are becoming accustomed to messaging about jobs across social channels. Recruiters can also use social media to build relationships with potential candidates and stay top of mind when they're ready to make a career move.

**They use employer branding to attract candidates.**

Employer branding has become increasingly important in recruiting. Candidates today want to work for companies with a strong brand and reputation, companies that will not only provide compensation for work but also create a chance to contribute to something bigger than any particular project or team. So, recruiting teams are focused on promoting their company's employer brand online and offline.

Employer branding includes company-sponsored events and meetups, blog or other social media posts about the company culture or values, and paid giveaways or tuition grants. Anything that helps other people learn about a company is beneficial for recruiters since those things draw people's attention and demonstrate what the company values most.

**They use the candidate experience to differentiate themselves.**

The candidate experience has become a key differentiator in recruiting. Candidates today have many choices and will only choose to work for companies that offer a great experience while interviewing. So, recruiting teams regularly focus on ensuring every touchpoint in the process is positive and memorable.

Each of these things are beneficial to recruiters and their teams, but they can also be beneficial for you as a designer looking to find a job and interview well.

If you know companies are relying on things like social media and employer branding to reach designers, be sure to look at a company's website and social channels to better understand what they're all about. Or if you know the company uses an ATS to screen applicants, make sure your resume is simple to parse and links to relevant experiences or examples of work that relate to a description on a job posting.

## 4. THE GOAL OF DESIGN INTERVIEWS

Most designers will have to undergo a job interview at some point in their careers. If you're reading this guide, my assumption is you are either new to interviewing or want to maximize your ability to interview well. The interviews you participate in aim to get to know you and your work better to determine if you are a good fit for the company. But the opposite is also true: interviews are a chance for you as a job candidate to determine if the company is the right fit for you.

Interviews are important because they allow employers to get to know potential employees on a personal level and assess their qualifications for the job. However, discussions can be challenging to conduct because they require both parties to be open and honest—and unbiased—which can be time-consuming and require some form of communication jiu-jitsu.

Design interviews can be challenging because they deal with outputs or artifacts of a very personal process. Recruiters and interviews often ask designers to share their work and discuss their strategies in retrospective and hypothetical scenarios to determine abilities as a result.

For some designers, these interviews can be frustrating and stressful, but understanding that companies want to ensure they're hiring someone who can not only show nice visuals or talk about design trends but do the job required. One of the most costly things for any business (and designer) is hiring someone who struggles to collaborate well, or who can't work in the way the company needs. Such scenarios result in poor company morale, delayed projects, and many moments of professional second-guessing.

The goal of interviewing is to ensure everyone involved can clearly and mindfully show their cards. When what's shared aligns, it's a chance to work together.

As an interviewee, invest as much as you feel comfortable evaluating the company you're interviewing. Ask tough questions about how the company supports designers and if they can provide examples of what effect work looks like at the company. Talk about times you've felt most proud of your work and times where you found yourself struggling; what context do you perform in the former and what would help you avoid the latter?

For an interview, you need to be prepared to discuss your skills, experience, and why you would be the best fit for the position. You can only do that if you also understand what the position is about, what the company is looking for, and what someone who gets the job will need to do in order to thrive. It's helpful also to come prepared with questions you can ask the company to understand what they value in their employees and whether or not they can provide you with the things you need to do your job well: compensation, learning and growth opportunities, space to do meaningful work, and so on.

There are a few things that employers typically want to know about designers during an interview. These include the designer's experience, education, portfolio, and design process. But they'll also want to understand how you work with others, what you value in your work, and how you prioritize competing opportunities. Employers can better understand you and your work by asking questions about these topics, but you should also look to asking the inverse of everyone you speak to while interviewing. How does the company collaborate? What does the company value most from teams? What does the prioritization and planning process look like at the company?

Experience conversations focus on your past work experiences. Employers want to know where you have worked and what kind of work you've done. Even if you have little-to-no formal design experience, talking about experience designing independent, school, or freelance projects, can give companies enough insight into your abilities. Similarly, sharing anecdotes of related experience—outside the world of design—can help make a great impression. Speak about the time you started a school club or led an effort to rally a group of friends toward a cause.

Something that is immediately helpful for companies to assess designers is past work. Employers want to see examples of real-world work to get a better sense of your style and skills. Having a digital portfolio can help you and recruiters communicate, as long as you tailor it to the specific job type you're interested in getting.

To understand your thought process and approach, employers want to know how you go about your work, where you shine, and where you struggle. Companies will also generally want to focus on interviewing your methods for designing products or solutions. However, be careful not to get too bogged down in the details. Your interviewer is likely more interested in the big picture of your design process than specifics about the software you use or the steps you take. Keep this in mind as you prepare for your interview and focus on providing a high-level overview of your process.

You will want to ask many questions throughout the interview process. Here are a few I recommend every designer asks early in the process to determine whether or not the company's hiring goal and your job goals are aligned:

1. What is the company's strategy for designing today? If they don't yet have a straightforward process, how do they plan to empower you to incorporate one?
2. What are the company's design principles or values? When making trade-offs, how do team members at the company decide what to prioritize and what to push off?
3. What challenges does the company face today related to design? In other words: why is this specific design role open, and why is the company hiring for it right now?
4. Who is involved in providing feedback to designers, and who is responsible for incorporating that feedback?
5. What projects might you work on in the first year of joining the company if you were to do so?

Now that you have a general understanding of recruiting, it's time to look closely into the job search process. Whether you're actively searching for a job or engaging with a recruiter or sourcer who has reached out to you, what follows is a large collection of insights that will help you throughout interviewing.

# TWO
# YOUR JOB SEARCH

## 1. WHY CAREER GOALS CAN BE VALUABLE FOR YOUR JOB SEARCH

Career goals can help you stay on track, keep you motivated, and make it easy to measure your professional growth. Your career goals can be big or small, near or far; what matters is that you often take a few short minutes to set and update them.

Career goals are what you want to achieve over time in your career. You can have short-term career goals (such as getting promoted or helping someone else with their goals) or long-term goals (like earning a certain amount of money or getting recognized as an expert).

Setting and regularly checking in on your goals matters because they can help you stay on track in your career, help you measure progress, and keep you motivated.

If goals sound intimidating or if you're the type of person who often neglects setting or following goals, have no worry. Your goals don't need to be something you spend a lot of time thinking about or developing (I'll explain a few processes you can use for coming up with your goal in the next few sections). Having some goal is often better than not having any; a vague goal can at least give you direction in the face of uncertainty or complexity. And if you have direction you're unlikely to remain stagnant, ungrowing, unimproved.

I firmly believe anyone interested in their career should have career goals. Especially if you're interviewing or looking for a job, having objectives can help you stay motivated and focused on what you want to achieve. A clear goal also gives you a clear topic of discussion while interviewing: you can ask questions and share your thoughts around your goal to keep conversations relevant and focused. If you don't have a goal for your career, any job can look like a promising one. Even the toxic jobs.

**Why you need a career goal.**

It can be easy to get complacent in a job or to view your less-than-nice job as something you must suffer through forever. Having a goal to work towards can help you stay motivated and focused on your career.

And again, it's important to note you don't need to set rigid and overly-detailed goals for your career. While project and business goals benefit from frameworks such as STAR (specific, testable, attainable, and relevant), career goals can be more ambitious and personal.

**A goal can also give you a sense of direction.**

It can be challenging to figure out what you want to do with your career—you might be overwhelmed by figuring out what jobs to search for or what jobs are worth pursuing—and having a goal can help you narrow down your options.

Additionally, **having a goal can help you stay organized and on-track.** It can be easy to get sidetracked when you don't have a clear goal in mind. Having a goal can help you stay focused on the overarching path of your career and ambitions, enabling you to avoid getting derailed by any new trend or shiny opportunity that comes your way that may or may not be good for you (and vice-versa).

**Having a goal can help you measure your progress and give you a sense of accomplishment.**

When you reach the later stages of your career: the expectation will be that you define achievements on your own, without waiting for someone else to define and celebrate them for you. Maybe you can already relate to this point with where you're at in your career.

Building a habit of defining achievements for yourself can start with your career goal. It can be challenging to tell if you're making progress in your career if you don't have a goal to measure against in the first place. Even if you don't reach your destination, working towards it can be rewarding as you take steps to develop.

**How career goals influence your job search.**

Having one or more defined career goals can be incredibly helpful when searching for a job.

Suppose your goal is to earn a high salary. In such a situation, you're likely to search for companies that pay more than average or use compensation as an initial talking point with companies you're interested in interviewing with. Or, if you want to work in a specific industry or as a designer at a certain level, you may search for jobs that are related to that industry or companies which openly advertise jobs at a certain level. These things affect your search even if you aren't cognitively aware of their influence.

Ultimately setting goals for your career is what determines the types of opportunities you are going to pursue. And if you don't have any career goals defined, you're more than likely to pursue any job that seems evenly remotely interesting, even if it won't be able to help you in your long-term career journey.

It's best if you are open to opportunities, of course, but over time you may find opportunities are plentiful and it's difficult to pick between them. Just as companies look for specific designers to fulfill their needs, you too should be looking for a particular match to where you're at in your career and the goals you have ahead of you.

Most people need to set career goals because it gives them a sense of direction and something to work towards often. Having goals also helps you stay motivated and focused on your career as you enter the interviewing process. It clarifies the types of opportunities to look for (e.g., will the job be able to support your goals?) and what to talk about during interviews.

With the value of career goals in-mind, it's time to think about what comes next for your career.

## 2. HOW TO DETERMINE CAREER GOALS

Setting career goals is a process that can be as simple or rigorous as you need it to be. What matters in determining your goals is how personal, actionable, and mutable you make them.

There are no universal best practices for determining career goals, and a goal-setting framework that works for someone else may not suit you. You do not need to have a bunch of goals at one time, and you don't need to target a specific time range for your career goals. Small, short-term plans can be just as effective as significant, long-term ones.

Because career goals are so personal, I don't recommend overthinking how you come up with them. Instead, you can generate meaningful career goals by looking at your skills, experiences, interests, and abilities and what actions you can take here and now.

**Evaluate your skills, experiences, and interests.**

To start figuring out what your career goals might look like, you need to assess your current skills, experiences, and interests.

What skills do you already have that you are proud of and want to hone further? Which skills do you wish you were better with, or what types of skills do you want to start developing that you don't yet have? Ask the same kinds of questions about your past experiences. What experiences have you found most rewarding that you hope to keep having in your career? What types of experiences do you want to try that you haven't? What experiences do you often see companies looking for in job posts or similar communications?

Though "things to avoid" can be informative, it's best to use "things to seek out" when creating goals. In other words: focus on goals around positives rather than negatives. Things you want more of offer a precise direction, whereas things to avoid are too general to create a plan.

If you're stuck on evaluating your skills, experiences, or interests, you can talk to friends, family, and teachers/managers to get their thoughts and advice. What's essential as you start determining career goals is figuring out what skills and experiences you've had that you want to keep and what skills you want to develop or pick up as determined by your interests and what you hear or see around you in the market.

**Consider what you can do with what you have now.**

Once you've identified a few skill or interest-related themes, you need to look at what actions you can take now related to them.

Any goal can be actionable, and what makes a career goal effective is focusing on the actions rather than the plan's outcomes. If you have a specific skill you want to learn, a great goal would be to *"figure out how [the skill] is often used by designers so you can decide if it's a skill you want to invest in yourself or change goals."*

If immediate action isn't explicit, that may indicate you need to rethink the subject of the goal itself. When in doubt, good first action can be as simple as *"figuring out what a first step might be."* Though the more specific and clear an activity is, the better the goal will be, since it's something you can move toward starting right now.

**Capture and track your goals (but don't sweat it).**

Writing things down makes them more tangible, sharable, and easy to reference. When we have ideas in mind, it's easy for them to change over time even without us wanting them to because that's how our minds work with abstract thoughts. We're more likely to forget things we store only in our minds.

Write down your career goal ideas and the goals you decide you'd like to work on starting now. Doing so will make them easier to look back to in the future, track your progress against, and share (with your manager, for example).

Additionally, consider doing the following for managing your career goals:

- Keeping a "work journal" that you update daily or weekly with minor updates toward your goals
- Sharing career goals and updates on social media

- Creating 5 minute, recurring "check-ins" with yourself on your calendar and spending the time reviewing your goals

**Embrace flexibility and adaptation.**

Mutable goals are most promising because they can be changed as needed. Goals that can easily change allow you to adapt to new circumstances and keep them relevant to your evolving interests, skills, and experiences.

Knowing that your career goals will have to adapt to changes should make it clear that setting any simple goal is more important than attempting to select idealistic ones.

Give yourself five minutes to reflect on what this guide has shared with you and see if you can develop a new career goal based on what you know about yourself, your skills, and your interests.

## 3. HOW TO IDENTIFY YOUR NEXT CAREER STEP

There is no one-size-fits-all or "best" career path for designers today. Instead, you have to figure out what the next step of your career might look like by evaluating your career goals, talking to others, and reminding yourself to be open to opportunities.

A career is what you do, over a significant period, with your skills and abilities. If you're just starting to figure out what your career might look like, the "next" step you take may be obvious: do what you can to put your skills to use however you can. But if you've held a job or two (or a dozen, as I have), or if you have studied design extensively, it can be daunting to think about what comes next.

Should you stay in your current field, move up the career ladder, or change fields? Should you keep growing in a specific skillset or work to be more of a generalist "do it all?" Is a job in people management essential to progress in your career, or is it enough to stay as an individual contributor who works hands-on in design every day? Many factors will influence the answers for you, and, despite what some people may want you to believe, there is no one-size-fits-all or "best" career path for designers.

When confronted with the question of "what should I look for in my next job?" designers have to decide between a myriad options. To figure out what the next step of your career might look like, you need to evaluate your career goals, skillset, interests, and what steps others before you have taken in their career.

Looking at your career goals is an excellent place to start evaluating the next step of your career. Your career goals do not have to answer the question of "what do I do next?" but can help you figure it out. If you find yourself setting lofty career goals that cover an extended period, your next career step might be to achieve those goals. If your goals are more focused on developing a specific skill or exploring a particular subject, the next step of your career will be some stepping stone toward that goal.

When deciding what your next career step looks like, it can be beneficial to talk with other designers who are a year or two at most more experienced than you.

Talking to someone more experienced than you can help you decide the next step of your career by giving you an outside perspective on your goals and how to best achieve them. Feedback and perspective from someone else can help you clarify what you want or need to do and how to do it. But speaking with someone who is ten years ahead of you may be less helpful, as that person is more inclined to misremember what they experienced in their career so long ago.

Of course, the more people you talk to about your career, the more options you will uncover for what your next step could look like and, as a result, what jobs to pursue. More conversations can help you learn about different job options, what steps you need to take to advance in your career, and what challenges you may face along the way (that you may or may not want to confront).

According to the US Bureau of Labor Statistics, designers change jobs every two years. You might change jobs more or less often than average, but it can be good to think of your career progression as a series of small steps rather than one of giant leaps. Remind yourself that any action you take in your career will be one of many. In fact: you aren't likely to get a "dream job" if you're starting your career—even if you do, odds are you'll want to continue learning and growing, so you will be looking for "that next step" eventually anyway.

Rather than being overwhelmed or afraid of defining what's next in your career, think of your next career step as a tiny change on a life-long journey of being able to develop and use your skills. And try not to tell yourself you can hold off on figuring out what your next career step might look like until the market or a company forces you to. Start now.

The next step for your career will be unique to you, but you can find it by setting career goals for yourself and talking with others about your goals, interests, experiences, and skills.

## 4. HOW TO FIND JOBS THAT ALIGN WITH YOUR GOALS

There are many ways for designers to find job opportunities today, from design job boards and communities, social networks, company websites, job fairs, design staffing agencies, and more. With so many options, finding the right job can be debilitating and exhausting. Thankfully, leveraging the ideal job search methods for your circumstances can help.

Believe it or not, the best way to find a job in design is not by Googling "design jobs near me" and applying to every job that looks promising. You *might* discover a great job that way, but odds are you'll burn yourself out and end up feeling more frustrated than fulfilled as rejections come into your inbox or your job applications go seemingly ignored.

A more effective way to find a job is to consider what role you're ready for in your career journey—based on your interests, skills, and professional goals. Then, research companies that align with your identified attributes by searching for them specifically and applying to them directly. You can also use the same signals those companies advertise for their jobs to expand your job search and hone your search criteria.

You want to find jobs that are not only interesting but which align with where you're at in your career and what you're hoping to do. Companies can quickly tell from a job application whether the person applying (the "candidate") is sending applications out to any and every job, or being thoughtful about their search. Recruiters will often look at your job application, résumé, and portfolio for critical indicators like language, education, or job experience (and more) to see whether things match up with the job description. So mass applying to jobs rarely works, try not to let such a fallible approach tempt you.

Your task when looking for a job is not merely applying to every possible position you see that *might* be good for you. Instead, it would be best if you put in a bit of work to find the jobs that align with your skills, experience, interests, and goals.

**Use your network like a pro.**

Whether you're just starting your career or looking for your 20th job: your network will be the best place to begin your search. But rather than telling your friends or acquaintances: "I'm looking for a design job, send me your referrals!", spend some time crafting your message for your network.

Write down what your career goal is and why it matters to you now. Add what skills you have and how you have used those skills in the past to help yourself or others achieve a goal. Expand your message by writing down example job posts you've found that look interesting and relevant, then ask if anyone knows of similar jobs that are open.

Many companies will use SEO—search engine optimization—to write job posts that reach a broad audience. To see what recruiters might be including in their job posts (and to see what keywords you might want to include in your search messaging) you can use a tool like ahrefs keyword generator or Google's Keyword Planner to find the most popular keywords.

Once you have a message you can share, post it where your network can readily see it. Then adapt the message to be custom for some of your closest friends. Explain, in a sentence or two, why you're asking them for help specifically and what they can do to help you: sharing any job posts they see, messaging any recruiters or hiring managers they know, or giving you feedback on your resume, portfolio, or outreach message itself.

**Look across job boards.**

Not every company advertises its open roles on job boards, but these boards are often a good indicator of what types of companies are actively hiring for specific positions. If you find a company that is interesting to you, apply to it through the job board, but also start looking for its competitors across sites like LinkedIn and Indeed to see if they are also hiring for similar roles.

Some job boards I recommend designers look at:

- LinkedIn
- Dribbble
- AuthenticJobs
- Read.cv
- Behance.net
- ArtStation

**Get full-time help.**

Apart from using your network to help you find job opportunities that align with your search, you may benefit from a staffing or recruiting agency. These companies work full-time to help place designers like you in roles. Because the staffing agency gets paid when you get a job, it can be advantageous to look to them for help. Not every staffing firm may be able to help you, but reaching out to these types of organizations can be worth trying.

Particularly if you have some years of experience, a design staffing firm might be a great resource to use while you search for jobs. These companies act as a bridge between designers like yourself and companies. They'll work with you and businesses to find a job that might be best suited for you.

Some example staffing agencies include:

- Creative People
- 80twenty
- Artisan

Once you've started to hone your job search, you can use the next section of this guide to evaluate job posts and identify the roles worth applying to (and which ones might be a waste of time).

## 5. EVALUATING JOB POSTS

Job posts are often vague and full of jargon or buzzwords and rely on repetitive formats to convey critically important information to job seekers. Because of this, you need to understand what job posts are trying to say and what makes them effective (or not).

A job post is typically an advertisement created by a company seeking to fill a specific position. A standard job post often includes details such as:

- Job title
- Brief job description
- List of required qualifications
- Statement about company culture or values
- Instructions on how to apply

Almost every sizable company uses job posts for advertising their open roles to a large audience. The more designers a company can reach with their job posts, the more likely they will be to find the best-suited person to fill them. And because job posts are self-filtering, they can be an excellent way for companies to find the optimal designer for their needs quickly.

Unfortunately, recruiters and hiring managers often write job posts, and while each is exceptional at communicating with and assessing designers, they are rarely formally trained on how to write well. As a result, most job posts can be problematic for designers to understand. You can be optimistic however, that job posts can provide incredible value to you in your search.

**What to look for in job posts.**

Many companies write job posts in a way that they hope will attract as many candidates as possible. As a result, you may see vague job postings that use certain words and phrases designed to catch your attention without being explicit.

When you're looking at a job post, pay close attention to things that can help clarify the intended audience and role expectations:

- **Specifics of the role—such as team or project details.** For example: "UX designer *on design systems*" or "creative lead *on social marketing.*"
- **Consistent and industry-used titles.** For example: "design unicorn" is exciting but unconventional and conveys a potential hazard in that the company is more interested in being catchy than clear, whereas a title like "product designer" is clear and familiar.
- **Examples of the job function, instead of a list of broad responsibilities.** For example: "Work closely with brand designers and sales partners to create a refreshed brand guide for customers" is an example of duty in action.
- **A long list of job qualifications presented as "must-haves" rather than "nice-to-haves."** Job posts with lengthy requirements alongside language like "ideally" or "nice to have" might be OK. Still, they may also communicate uncertainty around the role and how hiring managers will evaluate it.
- **Links to learn more.** Any additional information about a job is helpful information for you as a job seeker. Look for posts that include links to learn more about the design team, company culture, and anything that otherwise indicates the company appreciates good, thoughtful design practices (links to articles, awards, design team members on social channels, etc.).

A lack of these things should not be a deal-breaker for your job search, but each can help inform your evaluation of whether or not to apply to the role. Remember: the more specific you can be in your search, the more likely you are to get interviewed and, with some luck, the job.

**How to interpret a job post.**

To interpret a job post, start by looking at the job title. It sounds silly—of course, you're going to look at the job's title—but it's worth considering the seriousness of evaluating a job based on the title shared in a post. Clear and concise, conventional job titles are good. Titles with a small amount of additional detail (such as a team name or job objective) provide an immediate signal of what the company is looking for from candidates.

After the title, you should look immediately at the qualifications required. A best practice is: if you meet at least 60% of the qualifications listed, you should apply. Anything less can quickly determine the job isn't a good fit for you.

Pay special attention to your reaction to qualifications on job posts. According to Harvard Business Review, women tend to apply to jobs only when they meet 100% of the listed qualifications, while men apply if they meet just 60% of the requirements. You do not always need to meet 100% of the qualifications to be an excellent fit for a job. Though you should meet a minimum threshold of the requirements if you're to be seriously considered as a candidate.

If you feel good about the listed job requirements, move on to the job description. This section should give you a better idea of the day-to-day tasks that the job will entail, and it's here where you can evaluate your career goals, interests, abilities, and ambitions against the position. If the job description is too vague, or if it seems to focus more on selling the company than on the actual job duties, this could be a sign to move on to the next job post.

Finally, look at the company website and research the company culture, even if it's not listed directly in the job post. A little research on the company and its design team will give you a better idea of whether or not the company is a good fit for you and your career stage. If the company website is outdated, or if there is very little information available about the company and its design culture, this could be a sign that the company is not well-organized or that it is not a desirable workplace.

You could apply to every job you find that sounds somewhat promising, but by taking a closer look and seriously considering the attributes of the job post itself, you can save yourself a lot of time and headaches. By taking the time to interpret job postings, you can save yourself a lot of time and energy by applying for jobs that are a good fit for you.

# 6. LEVERAGING YOUR NETWORK TO FIND JOBS

Looking for a job can be a daunting task. Luckily, many resources are available to help you search for job opportunities that align with your goal, skills, and ambitions. One of the most important resources at your disposal is your personal network.

Your network comprises of the people you know and interact with regularly, including family, friends, acquaintances, and your online connections. These people can be a great resource when you're looking for a job because they may know of openings that are not yet public or stumble across a job that would be good for you.

Your connections are people who can help you find leads on job openings, advise your job search, and provide moral support during the process. You can expand your search exponentially by leveraging your network. But how do you best utilize your network to help with your search? Here are a few tips for using your network to find a job:

1. Talk to people you are closest to in your network about your job search. Let them know what you're looking for and ask if they know of any openings or would keep an eye out for them.
2. Ask close contacts if they're willing to introduce you to someone who works in your desired industry or company. (Do not ask this of strangers, as many professionals do not feel comfortable recommending or introducing people they do not know well to others.)
3. Use social media to connect with your network. Post about your job search and ask if anyone knows of any openings that might be good to pursue.
4. Attend networking events. Recruiting events like a company happy hour, job fairs, or local meetups can be a great way to meet new people and expand your network.
5. Be willing to help out your contacts. If someone in your network is also looking for a job, offer to help them with their search.

Utilizing your personal network will increase your chances of finding a job. Two additional points are worth noting:

**Be specific and provide an overview for others to reference.**

The more specific your search, the more likely you are to find a role that aligns with where you are at in your career. Mainly when using your network to help you in your job search: the more specific you can be, the better.

Prepare to message you can use and ask others to share around what type of role you are looking to get. What job title are you hoping to get from your search? What skills do you offer, and what are you trying to do with them? Are you open to on-location, remote, or hybrid work? Is there a specific team or company culture you're eager to find?

**Focus on close, connected friends and acquaintances.**

Try not to ask everyone you can for help. Instead, select a handful of people you are close with who also are well-connected. Think of their help as an investment, something to keep tabs on regularly and check in on as you continue searching. People are busy, and even the most well-intentioned among us can forget to follow up.

Additionally, if you can, offer something in return for others' help. A lunch out together or a nice gift can go a long way to show gratitude for someone's assistance—even if they're only able to keep their eyes open for jobs that may be a good match for your search.

Once you've got a sense for where to look for jobs, how to evaluate posts, and how to leverage your network for support, it's time to seriously evaluate your résumé.

# 7. WHY YOU NEED A RÉSUMÉ

Résumés are important to have, even in today's mostly digital world, because they provide others with a simple snapshot of your skills, experience and qualifications. In a competitive job market, a well-written résumé can give you a distinct advantage over other designers.

A résumé—a shareable document outlining your past experience and expertise—is often one of the first points of contact between you and a hiring company. Your résumé is how a recruiter or hiring manager will first assess whether you are a potential match for a job. It's important to make a good impression and convey key information about your background and qualifications in a concise and easy-to-read format, and a résumé allows you to do just that.

Because résumés are often text-based and offer a lot of information in a condensed format, they're easy to share and review. Meaning: unlike a design portfolio, a website, or a social feed, a résumé can be emailed to anyone, viewed on almost any device, and visually scanned or skimmed for relevant information (including, ideally, the ability for someone to command+F and search the résumé).

If you're still unsure whether you need a résumé or not, consider this: it's better to have a résumé and not need it than need one and not have it. A simple résumé can go a long way in your job search, and also offer a lot more that you might not initial consider, such as:

**A résumé can help you track your accomplishments.**

It can be easy to forget about all the things you've done over the course of your career. Having a résumé handy can help you remember all your accomplishments and feel more confident when networking or applying for new opportunities.

**Résumés can help you stand out.**

In today's competitive job market, it's more important than ever to make sure your resume stands out from the rest. By creating a simple, straight-forward résumé, you can showcase your unique skills and experience and make a strong impression on potential employers.

**Résumés can be a valuable networking tool.**

When meeting new people or pulling in help in your job search, it's always helpful to have a copy of your résumé. This way, you can quickly and easily give people an overview of your professional background and skills. Your resume can also be a helpful starting point for conversations about potential job opportunities.

Store a copy of your résumé in a cloud service provider like iCloud or Google Drive so you can always access or share a link to it. (Personally, I refer people to my LinkedIn profile and use that as my résumé. The website allows anyone to save a profile as a more scannable PDF.)

**Résumés can help you prepare for interviews.**

When you're getting ready for a job interview, your resume can be a valuable tool for preparing answers to common interview questions. Reviewing your resume before an interview can help you refresh your memory on your qualifications and accomplishments.

Overall, résumés are an important part of the job search process. Whether you're looking for a new job or trying to network with new contacts, having a well-written résumé can make a big difference.

## 8. HOW TO WRITE AN EFFECTIVE RÉSUMÉ

Résumés are important, but how do you create one that stands out while also not being overwhelming? What information should you include and what information is unnecessary is a hot topic, and many people tend to overestimate the value of certain subjects on a résumé.

To write an effective résumé, first consider what a résumé isn't. A résumé is not a list of everything you have ever done in your career. It's best not to treat your résumé as a life biography or a comprehensive record of your awards, accolades, or skills either. A résumé is a tool to market your relevant skills and experiences for a specific type of job, plain and simple.

The purpose of a résumé is to sell your professional self. The goal of your résumé should be to provide enough information about yourself to entice a recruiter or hiring manager to engage with you and learn more.

**What to include in your résumé,.**

A typical design résumé should include:

- Your name and contact information (including your phone number, email address, and url of a design portfolio—and portfolio password if applicable).
- A one-to-two sentence introductory summary of your relevant skills and experience, or why you're "ideal for the job."
- A list of your professional experience, including the names of the companies you worked for, your job title, dates of employment, and at most five bullet points listing examples of what you accomplished in the role.
- A list of your education and training (if applicable).
- A list of any notable professional memberships and awards (if applicable).

There is no need to include information that is irrelevant to the job or would not be of interest to the employer. This includes your hobbies, non-career-related skills, beliefs or philosophies, etc. Save that information for the interview or your personal website and let your résumé be simple but effective at what it needs to do. With that in mind, here's how to write a résumé to help you get the job you want.

**Keep your résumé concise.**

The average résumé is just one or two pages long at most. Employers are busy and often have to review dozens or even hundreds of résumés daily. Companies do not want to read a novel about your life and work; they want to know if you are qualified for the job and need to determine that quickly. So keep your resume concise and to the point.

With limited time to read and review each résumé, recruiters need to be able to assess your skills and experience quickly. A concise résumé is good, and a plain-text one is best. Examples of your past experience will be the core of your résumé, anything else should be considered noisy.

Additionally, avoid trying to over-design your résumé and instead consider a single-column, plain-text document with solid use of headers, lists with indentation, and bold/italic styling.

**Note:** Tools like Grammarly.com can help proofread and simplify your résumé!

**Share brief experiences and examples.**

Employers want to see what you have accomplished, not just what your job duties were or what your interests are. Highlight your achievements and experiences in each position, and include numbers whenever possible. For example, *"Designed the company's first marketing outreach campaign on social media and paid ads, which increased sales by 25% in six months"* is much more informative for recruiters than *"Designed brand campaigns sales."*

A common mistake I see designers make is adding a section to their résumé with a list of their design skills. Writing skills as a list on your résumé does not tell recruiters how you use those skills or whether you really possess them—as anyone can write a bulleted list of keywords they found when searching for "designer skills" on Google. Instead, write a single sentence example of a time you had to use a skill for a specific job. Rather than writing out a list of skills, use bolded skill keywords in samples of your experience.

When describing your work experience and accomplishments, use strong action verbs at the start of each bullet, such as "developed," "designed," "implemented," "managed," etc. Strong verbs will make your résumé more powerful and easier to read. These verbs also enforce you to think about your contributions and the ways you use your skills on the job.

Do try to use the same keywords you see used to describe skills and responsibilities in job posts. Recruiting software will parse your résumé for these keywords and visually call attention to it for recruiters, while design hiring managers will manually skim your résumé to see if these skill words appear. Listing skills outright is a no-no, but including skill words in your example statements can be powerful.

As a final example, rather than saying, *"Skilled in prototyping and customer research,"* you might say, *"Have used interactive Figma prototypes to evaluate customer comprehension of new user onboarding."*

**Think of your résumé as one piece of a larger whole**

Recruiting teams will often want to see your résumé before looking at your portfolio of work. But they may also glance at any social profiles you share and compare each of these things to determine your skills, experience, and ambitions. It's meaningful to align your résumé with other ways you present yourself to hiring companies.

If your résumé says you are an experienced brand designer, but your portfolio lists you as a "passionate marketing designer" and your LinkedIn title is "aspiring UX/brand designer," you send mixed signals to recruiting teams. This weakens your overall message and can confuse recruiters. Make sure the way you present yourself is always consistent.

Finally, ensure your résumé is always up to date with your latest experience and achievements. Please do not wait until you are looking for a job; update it regularly as you progress in your career.

Writing a good résumé is an essential step in your job search journey. By following these tips, you can be sure that yours will stand out from the rest and help you get the interviews you want.

# Jacquline Varela

Senior Visual Designer

Email: jacqulinevarela@emaildomain.com
Portfolio: jacqulinevareladesign.domain.com
Phone: + 1 987-654-3210

## About me

With more than three years of experience designing visual graphics for websites, events, and small businesses, I have what it takes to understand customer needs and translate them into solid conversion metrics. I am looking for my next role as a senior visual or graphic designer, ideally on a team where I can work more closely with user experience designers to take my visual craft and apply it to more product areas.

## Experience

**Senior graphic designer**
PCL Design Studio (www.pclfakedesign.com) - Full time
Remote
February 2022 - Current

- Created twelve large marketing campaigns alongside the company art team. Many campaigns included the design of printed materials (magazine and mailers), online adverts (banners, page takeovers, sponsored publication content), and more.
- Led creative brainstorming sessions and ideation exercises with a team of twelve designers, developers, and project managers, resulting in the design and launch of a new website for a fortune 50 company.
- Established new creative guidelines for Nike, with help from six creative and content leads. Brought complex concepts for how to present infographic data in a web interface to life.
- Won two awards for my creative direction and team guidance on an 80-page website design for Pepsi Co.

**Graphic designer**
Locré - Full time
San Francisco, California, United States
January 2020 - February 2022

- Led design on several international digital advertising campaigns, including three ads in time square for Nike, two of which won an internal company award for the "Best Creative ad ideas" award in 2021.
- Worked with two copywriters and six developers to develop new website assets for global brand clients, including Gap, Lacoste, McDonalds, and Red Bull, leading to a total of 2,580,000 web views for these customers since 2020.
- Partnered with company marketing director to envision and create a new and faster process of making customer site maps in Figma using shared visual component libraries.
- Worked with three senior front-end developers, a copywriter, and a product manager to write and share guides customers could use for onboarding to Webflow with our delivered design assets.

## Education and certification

**Academy of Art University**
Master of Fine Arts - MFA, The School of Graphic Design - May 2020

**School of Visual Arts**
CPE [Continuing Professional Education], Graphic Design - June 2022

*Example résumé*

## 9. GETTING FEEDBACK ON YOUR RÉSUMÉ

It's a good idea to get feedback on your résumé to identify errors, improvements, and anything that might be unclear to others. But before you ask a friend for feedback, consider taking it to someone with hiring experience.

It's valuable to get feedback on your résumé before sending it to employers because doing so allows you to make sure your résumé is clear, concise, and free of errors or confusing language. You don't need to have many people review your résumé, nor do you have to pay for a professional review, but having one or two people take a look at your résumé will help increase your chances of getting an interview.

Ideally, you can get feedback on your résumé from someone with hiring experience: a design recruiter, hiring manager, or simply a designer who has been part of a hiring panel and process at a company. Those with hiring experience can tell you what looks good and what you can improve. You can also ask for feedback from friends or family members, but they may not be as objective as someone with hiring experience.

What if you don't know anyone who has previously worked in the hiring process? You *can* pay a professional service to review your résumé, but doing so does not always guarantee someone with design hiring experience will check it.

Additionally, you can ask friends, family, and colleagues/peers if they know of any good recruiters you could reach out to for feedback. Recruiters are often very busy, but they also enjoy helping job seekers maximize their potential, and reviewing résumés is one (relatively lightweight) way for them to help. So consider looking for a recruiter in your network (on a site such as LinkedIn) and politely asking them if they could help you. Do not spam multiple recruiters asking for feedback, however, as you will only come across as desperate and annoying rather than eager to learn and improve.

No matter who you go to for résumé feedback, make sure to ask specific questions, such as:

- Is the layout easy to read and understand?
- Is there too much or too little information?
- What weaknesses does the résumé immediately convey? What strengths?
- Do the examples provided clarify how I have utilized my skills?
- Are there glaring things that I should add or remove?

Feedback on your résumé can be crucial in creating a solid document to help you get the job you want. So don't be afraid to ask for a little help and incorporating the feedback you receive.

## 10. HOW A PORTFOLIO CAN HELP YOUR JOB SEARCH

If a résumé is a must-have for a job search, a strong portfolio of work is a superpower.

A design portfolio is one of a designer's most important tools when searching for a job. A portfolio of work allows you to showcase your skills and experience to others in a lightweight, easy-to-share, and understand way. What makes design portfolios most valuable for designers looking for a job is that a portfolio can work without you: companies can find, reference, and explore your portfolio without you in the room or needing to be on a call. Because of this ability to "work for you" when you aren't there, a clear yet detailed portfolio of work is a worthwhile investment to make.

Most employers require designers to submit a portfolio as part of the job application process anyway. This is because a portfolio allows others to see and explore examples of your work efficiently and to get an idea of the skills and experience you would bring to a job.

A compelling portfolio is a collection of work showcasing your skills and abilities. It will demonstrate your experience, style, and capabilities. A recruiter or hiring manager can look at your work portfolio and determine whether you would be a match for what they need on their team.

As a result, a portfolio is often an essential tool for designers to use when applying for jobs, no matter their level of experience. It allows you to show off your best work and make an impression on potential employers without you needing to voice over everything you've done to every company repeatedly.

Additionally, a well-designed portfolio can make the difference between getting a job and not getting one. A designer with a portfolio of work will be able to more clearly and succinctly communicate their skills—since they've already done the leg work of defining a story, or case study, for their experience. In contrast, a designer without a portfolio may be able to impress with a résumé or set of experiences but might struggle to speak to a concrete set of skills. And when a recruiter needs to reference past work, not having a portfolio can make that process tricky or even impossible for them.

When in doubt: create a portfolio of your work. Not having a portfolio means companies have to invest more time and energy in figuring out whether or not a designer has the skills or attributes required to do a job.

Lastly, having a digital portfolio in the form of a website or as part of a design community such as Dribbble or Behance means hiring companies can find you and your work more efficiently: by searching for designers with your skills or experiences. Designers without a portfolio won't appear in Google search results, won't be as easy to remember, and will need to be engaged more often with the recruiting team to get answers or details of their past work.

I hope it's clear at this point how a portfolio can be essential for designers looking for jobs because it is a way to showcase their work, skills, and experience quickly. You can build a portfolio website from scratch, by using Figma, or through a site builder such as Squarespace, Adobe Portfolio, Wix, or my personal favorite tool, Webflow.

## 11. WHAT TO INCLUDE IN A DIGITAL PORTFOLIO

When creating a solid portfolio, it's best to create a visually appealing and informative space. Remember, the purpose of a digital portfolio is not to get you a job. The objective is to get you an interview. Giving recruiters, hiring managers, and designers at hiring companies information in a discoverable, easy-to-navigate, and simple-to-understand way is vital.

So we're on the same page: a digital portfolio is any digital collection of your design work. If the goal of an effective portfolio is to catch the interest of a hiring team, what you include must be essential to that purpose. Your portfolio should provide enough context and examples to entice a recruiter or hiring manager to want to interview you. Anything you include in your portfolio that detracts from what a hiring team is looking for may hinder your ability to capture their interest and get an interview.

Additionally, a well-designed portfolio can set the stage for the rest of your work as a designer, but it should not be a project in and of itself. Your portfolio does not need to take a lot of time to create, and you do not need to include every piece of work you've done. Nor do you need to make your portfolio overly stylish or littered with superfluous details in the name of being "unique."

What should go into your portfolio?

Before exploring what to include in your design portfolio, it's worth noting that looking to other designers' portfolios for ideas is not always helpful. Where someone is at in their career and what they have as their career goals may be different than your own. My portfolio website may look great to recruiters but overly plain to other designers. Someone else's portfolio may have been built to accommodate their desire to speak at conferences and not help them at all with getting a job. Instead of looking at other's portfolios for inspiration, please focus on the first principles of what it is you want your portfolio to accomplish and build it from there.

That said, here are the most fundamental elements a portfolio should include:

**1. Include an engaging and well-designed homepage.**

Your homepage is essentially the "face" of your portfolio, so you need to make it visually appealing and easy to navigate. The first page someone sees when visiting your portfolio should be an index of where you want them to look next, making it easy for visitors to access all of your work with one or two clicks at most from the homepage.

**Note:** For my portfolio website I include examples of multiple projects directly on the homepage. That way recruiters or hiring managers can get an immediate feel for my work, but also "click into" each work experience to learn more about my work through detailed case studies.

Avoid cluttered designs and overwhelming amounts of text—instead, opt for a clean and minimalistic approach that highlights your best work in a concise and visually-appealing way (remember to check that your portfolio meets accessibility requirements, tools like Stark can help).

You can set the stage for those who visit your portfolio by mentally "priming" them on your homepage: use clear and concise language that aligns with what you are looking for in your job search. Use that same language across your résumé and social profiles to create a consistent and robust digital presence. This way, no matter where a recruiter encounters you, the message will be the same: *"I am this type of designer with these types of skills looking to do this type of work."*

You can use free keyword search tools to identify what words are most commonly associated with design portfolios. Or you can look at job posts across sites like LinkedIn, Dribbble, and AuthenticJobs, and see what language recruiting teams use that you can then include in your homepage and throughout your portfolio.

**2. Include a variety of work samples.**

When showcasing your work, it's essential to include a variety of samples that highlight both the breadth and depth of your skillset.

Have both individual pieces and larger projects, and make sure to showcase a variety of mediums, styles, and techniques.

Think deeply about the order of projects you show and how you interconnect each project on your portfolio, as recruiting teams won't have enormous amounts of time to explore the entirety of your portfolio.

In addition to visual samples, your portfolio should include detailed descriptions of your past work. These descriptions should provide an overview of the project and highlight your specific role and contributions (refer to the next section of this chapter on how to write a case study for your portfolio).

One tip I always recommend for designer portfolios is not merely listing things like your role, timeline, and skills used in your work samples. Too often designers think that listing the team members you worked with at the top of a case study is sufficient, but as with listing skills on your résumé: a plain list doesn't tell others how you actually worked with those people listed. Instead: find ways to incorporate those details directly into the work sample descriptions.

For example, share a real-life example of your interactions with team members rather than listing out a team you worked with: *"I worked closely with a project manager and lead engineer early in the project to determine goals. Once we landed on a few hypotheses together, I presented the goals to our VP of Product one-on-one to get their feedback. The resulting goals shaped how I explored early design concepts."*

**3. Incorporate an organized and easy-to-navigate layout.**

Your portfolio website should be easy to navigate, with a clear and concise layout that allows recruiters and hiring managers to find the information they are looking for quickly and easily.

Avoid complex navigation menus and overwhelming page layouts or "interstitial" pages that serve no purpose apart from adding noise to your portfolio. Instead, focus on creating a straightforward user experience. As visitors to your portfolio won't have a lot of time to browse and explore, the simpler and more interconnected you can make the hierarchy of your portfolio website, the better it will be at helping you land an interview.

**Note:** Does your portfolio need to work across devices types, including smartphones or tablets? If you want to ensure your portfolio is accessible and useful for the widest array of possible scenarios, it's a good idea to make sure it works well on mobile devices. However, it's certainly not a hard requirement, as most of the time hiring managers and recruiters will be reviewing your portfolio from a sizable monitor and desktop hardware. More on this point in the upcoming sections around designing and building your portfolio.)

**4. Add a concise way to learn about you.**

When looking for job candidates, recruiting teams often want a glimpse of the person behind the work. It's best if you do not write a biography about yourself. Still, you should create a space in your portfolio for a few sentences about yourself and your background, as well as links to how to contact you (by email or social media, for example) and how someone can learn more about you if they wanted to.

Including links to any social accounts you feel comfortable sharing is a great way to give recruiting teams a small look into your identity and interests, but by no means is including social links a requirement to have in your portfolio.

**What about including hobbies, extracurriculars, awards, and references?**

Some people believe that including hobbies such as writing, public speaking, and photography in a portfolio can be a waste of space and a detractor from your primary skills.

Others believe the more you include about yourself and your interests, the more you present a well-rounded view to those who visit your portfolio.

Both perspectives are valid, and both options—including non-design-related details or not—have downsides. A simple way to determine whether to include something in your portfolio or not is this: if what you're adding can be immediately understood concerning the work you want to be doing in your career, include it in your portfolio.

In other words: if you want to highlight how your experience in some different realm has influenced your work, that is worth considering in your portfolio. Photography, programming, painting, sculpture, lecturing or teaching, writing, and architecture, are all ways someone can use design-related skills and could therefore be worth including in your portfolio.

In contrast, if what you're including is immediately apparent in how it relates to your design career, it's better to exclude it from your portfolio. It's great if you love activities like yoga, travel, hiking, or playing video games, but those things are not likely to benefit your career directly, so do not highlight them.

## 12. HOW TO WRITE A CASE STUDY

Knowing what will go in your portfolio is a good start, it's a way to build the foundations of the portfolio. Looking back at what the core of your portfolio should entail, I hope it's apparent that the heart of any portfolio is the design work itself. Rather than adding a few photos of your design work and calling it a day, consider instead writing a case study for your past work experiences.

Case studies are essential to any portfolio, allowing you to showcase your work thoughtfully and contextually. A case study should demonstrate your ability to solve problems, collaborate with others, and think beyond the visuals of what it is you design.

In other words: a case study is a presentation method adapted by creative professionals and involves an in-depth, detailed look at a specific project.

In academics, where the case study format originates, case studies are usually research projects conducted over time and often involve interviews and other forms of data collection and synthesis. The case study method is powerful because it allows researchers to study something—a person, business, or project—in its natural environment. This allows for a more in-depth understanding of the subject than possible if the research is conducted using a more rigid or controlled method.

With this framing in mind, you can see how a case study for something like a work sample in your design portfolio should be an organic, natural presentation of what the work entailed. When you think of your past experiences in terms of a case study—a research-like evaluation of your work—it can serve many purposes, including helping you to mentally solidify the story you tell yourself and others about your work.

You can use case studies to show off your skills and highlight the impact of your work in a way that feels comfortable to you. When done well, a case study is a potent communication tool in addition to a resource for recruiters and hiring teams, making it an optimal way for recruiters to learn about your design skills as well as how you communicate around your work.

When writing a case study for your portfolio, it's vital to showcase your work in a real-world context. Rather than attempting to follow a strict format for your case study—such as the cliché Problem > Empathize> Research > Ideate > Test > Implement format—construct each case study to represent the reality of the work you participated in as part of the project. What really happened, in what order, and why?

For example, if a project began with your boss asking you to look into a customer complaint, your case study should start at that prompt and your reaction to it—how did you feel when your boss asked to begin the work? What was your immediate response to the request? What did you want to do first, and why?

If your case study is honest about the reality of what happened, it will convey the skills and experiences that are unique to you. It will also be much more interesting to read! Recruiters do not want to see the same case study format for every portfolio they visit; they want to see what happened, what you did for the project, and a brief explanation for why you did what you did at each step.

So how do you go about writing a compelling case study? Here are some tips:

**1. Choose a project you're passionate about or which was personally impactful.**

When writing a case study, choosing a project you're passionate about or that impacted you is the most important thing. This will allow you to write with conviction and tell a more compelling story.

Projects that were impactful to you will readily come to mind: any project that caused you to reflect on your beliefs, processes, or abilities or a project you developed professionally or personally are great projects to start with for writing. As you write your case study, you will want to hone in on the moments of the project that allowed you to learn or grow the most.

A project where you had to learn a new way to adapt your skill makes for the best type of case study because it will show recruiting teams how you apply and evolve your skills as a designer.

**2. Keep it concise,**

A case study should be concise and to the point. There's no need to waffle on—get straight to the point and explain what you did, how you did it, and what the results were.

An optimal format for your case study might look something like this:

- Project or company title.
- Introduction paragraph about the project and what it meant for you.
- Your story working on the project, from beginning to end.
- Summary or recap of your story and the outcomes.
- A link to a similar / next case study to explore.

Too often, designers will start their case study by giving a comprehensive overview of the business they were working for as part of the project. This information does not matter as much as you might think it does for recruiters. Instead, recruiters want to get straight to your personal experience working on the project, so starting your case study with your personal situation is essential.

An excellent exercise to develop case studies—for your digital portfolio or as part of a portfolio presentation—is to craft a narrative as if you were talking to a close friend about the project.

If you had 30 minutes to sit down with a friend and tell them about a specific project you worked on, what would you tell them? What would you highlight for them, and how would you phrase it? Whatever you come up with: that's most likely the best outline you can use for your portfolio case studies.

**3. Use plenty of visuals.**

Remember that a picture is worth a thousand words, particularly in design: a visual-heavy medium. Use plenty of case study visuals to show off your work. Include before-and-after shots, screenshots, infographics, photos of your notes and sketches, videos or animated GIFs of your prototypes or presentations, and anything else that will help to tell your story.

Even parts of your story that don't deal with design artifacts will likely have a visual component. Screenshots of Slack conversations (edited to hide sensitive information), photos of Zoom calls with customers, whiteboards, wireframes, and notebook scribbles can all be great ways to tell part of the story visually.

**4. Be honest.**

When writing a case study, it's important to be honest about both the successes and the failures. Don't try to gloss over any problems— instead, explain how you overcame them. This will show that you can think on your feet and come up with creative solutions when things get tough.

Your case study should begin with your personal experience and end with it. If the project ended suddenly when leadership cut resources at your company, say as much. If the project was a huge success and had the CEO raving about it, mention that. The important thing for writing a case study is to write *your story*.

**5. Get feedback.**

Before you publish your case study, it's a good idea to get feedback from design recruiters or hiring managers if possible. They may be able to spot errors or omissions you've missed, and their input can help to improve the final piece.

Writing a case study doesn't have to be a daunting task. Following these simple tips can create a compelling piece showing off your skills and experience.

## 13. HOW TO DESIGN A DIGITAL PORTFOLIO

At this point you should have a clear understanding of why a digital portfolio is beneficial to have in your job search, the structure of your portfolio, as well as how to construct case studies to share your work experience. What comes next is figuring out how to design your portfolio to demonstrate your taste, as well as skills and experience.

A digital portfolio should be visually pleasing, representative of your work, easy to navigate, and user-friendly. To accomplish all this, design your portfolio in a way that highlights the work itself and allows it to shine.

While you can turn your portfolio into a piece of work, you do not need to spend excessive time crafting and designing it. Recruiters and their team will rarely use the superficial elements of a portfolio as a signal of whether a designer is capable or not—there are exceptions to this point, of course. Having a great-looking portfolio can be supplementary, but recruiters will typically opt to look more closely at your work as an indicator of your abilities since that's where you'll have confronted real-world constraints, timelines, collaboration needs, etc.

Unless you're interested in jobs designing portfolios for other designers, it's best to focus on keeping your portfolio simple, concise, and straightforward. Let your work experience be what sets you apart from everyone else.

Not every designer has the time to invest in designing a fancy portfolio, and that's ok. Go ahead if you have interest and time to build a dynamic portfolio. But know that any value your portfolio may give to impressing visitors will be minuscule compared to your work and experience you include in your portfolio. In the end, it's work examples that ultimately sell your skills: they're real examples of how you work with others on real-world constraints and needs, whereas your portfolio may be simply an expression of what you enjoy doing. However, a little polish on your portfolio doesn't hurt either.

By creating a portfolio that highlights your unique strengths and abilities through your work in a way that is easy to navigate and explore, you can provide those coming to your portfolio precisely what they're looking for: broad and deep examples of your work.

When designed well, your portfolio will work for you: you won't need to explain what's on it or elaborate to someone during a meeting. The work will be clear and convey your skills and abilities effectively. With all that in mind, here are the most critical things to focus on when designing your portfolio.

**Design it to be easily navigable.**

The most crucial aspect to consider when designing a portfolio is keeping things organized and making it easy for visitors to find what they're looking for while browsing.

Visitors to your portfolio will want to see a wide variety of work if possible, and anything you can do to help them quickly navigate projects helps them accomplish that. Additionally, ensuring visitors can quickly jump between projects, an about me section, and contact or learn more areas (if you choose to include them) will increase the likelihood of them investing more time in evaluating it.

If you have less than a handful of projects, you do not need a separate homepage and "work" page, for example. Find a creative way to make your homepage and work overview page with links to each case study.

Or, if you have a blog on your website and many projects, you can incorporate "Look at this next" links to the top and bottom of each case study or blog post to give visitors suggested actions (and quick access) to more of your work.

**Make it reflective of your style.**

Choose a design for your portfolio that is visually appealing and representative of your work. Particularly if you do not have a lot of work yet, your portfolio can convey to others the type of work you want to design.

If you're interested in creative game design, your portfolio might be more colorful and unconventional than other portfolios. Or, if you're interested in designing for a company like Apple, your portfolio should be clean and straightforward.

Adding small touches of personal "brand" to your portfolio can convey a lot about you and your work; make sure what elements you add also reflect your position in the portfolio. If your portfolio is flashy and colorful, but your work is bland and dry, others looking through it may be confused about your capabilities.

**Focus on the visuals.**

You may be inclined to write a lot of information for your case studies. Much written communication can be valuable in some cases (such as incredibly complex workflows). However, because so much of the work we do as designers ultimately leads to a visual or engaging experience, it's best to show that work in your portfolio.

You can even use visuals to spotlight non-visual steps of your case study: screenshots showing your notes or a photo of you talking to customers or stakeholders. You can use these photos alongside things like wireframes, screenshots of your prototyping setup, hand-drawn explorations, etc., to convey your design process visually rather than written. And because visual artifacts are more concrete than written anecdotes, they're more believable as demonstrations of a process.

Recruiters will likely view your portfolio in many different ways on devices such as iPads, laptops, and desktop computers, so you want to use clear high-quality images. Avoid low-resolution photos or images that are not easy to zoom into to see design details.

Some additional tips for designing the visuals in your portfolio:

- Avoid using images of grids or tiled designs; doing so makes it harder to see the details of your design.
- Avoid overusing "chrome" in designs: the stuff around your work that you did not design yourself, such as web browser interfaces, phone mockups, or real-life settings.

- Use animated gifs or short video clips if you have work involving animation, motion, or interaction design (where users must navigate through an experience).
- Use images that can easily be zoomed into or magnified to evaluate your design decisions.
- Do use multiple images to draw attention to specific details in your work. For example: showing one picture of a complete design, then a second image which is a detailed and highly magnified element of the full design.

## 14. HOW TO BUILD YOUR PORTFOLIO

Because a portfolio is a collection of work, ideally presented as extensive case studies, it's intuitive that you would build it using something that makes your portfolio easy to discover, explore or navigate, share, and interpret.

I always recommend designers build their portfolio as a website, for numerous reasons. Recruiters and hiring managers can discover a website through search engines and share it easily through email or social channels. A website portfolio offers flexibility on how users navigate it and, if built well, works across various devices and operating systems. You can't get those same benefits through a prototype, presentation deck, or PDF. For these reasons, I recommend creating a portfolio using a website.

You can quickly build a website portfolio by using a platform such as WordPress, Squarespace, Webflow, or Wix. Another option is to create an online portfolio using a service such as Behance, Adobe Portfolio, Cargo, or Dribbble (which supports full case study projects). If you really wanted to you could even use Notion to build your portfolio.

Each of these platforms allows you to create a profile and upload your work in a responsive and modern way, without much overhead. You do not need to learn how to program to make a compelling portfolio, and most recruiting teams don't care much for custom-built portfolios over generator-built ones.

It would be best if you did not worry about re-using a popular website template or whether your portfolio is "unique" enough for your job search. Your work is what needs to be unique, not necessarily your portfolio itself. Spend your energy on writing your case studies and building your portfolio, and less time worrying about whether it looks too similar to everyone else's.

Another way to build a digital portfolio is to create a blog or vlog (video blog) dedicated to your work. Platforms such as WordPress and Tumblr make it easy to create a blog, and there are many video hosting platforms such as YouTube, Vimeo, and Wistia, where you can upload videos walking through your work. A blog or video collection can be a great way to share your work with recruiting teams, build a personal brand around your work and interests, and build an audience who can help you find a job.

A downside to using a format like video for a portfolio is that it limits navigation across your work. A collection of videos makes it difficult for a recruiter to jump around your case studies to pick up a signal specific to the job they're hiring. Though, with features such as YouTube video chapters, you can add a level of navigation to videos that make them more dynamic and accessible if video speaks to you as your portfolio medium of choice.

Finally, you can also use social media to build a digital portfolio—at least as supplementary pieces to a more extensive portfolio website. Platforms such as Twitter, LinkedIn, and Pinterest allow you to share images and videos of your work with a broad audience, and you can often include enough context in those posts to help others learn about your work. Having a social media following can also be a great way to attract new clients or employers. Though, just as with video format portfolios, navigating a social media profile is cumbersome compared to a website designed for your work.

No matter which method you choose to build a portfolio, remember that a digital portfolio is a great way to showcase your skills and attract new opportunities. Done is better than perfect, and having a portfolio when you don't think you need one is better than not having one when it turns out you do.

## 15. PULLING EVERYTHING TOGETHER FOR YOUR PORTFOLIO

When you know how you want to build your portfolio and you're ready to start designing and assembling it (or already have), it's good to briefly pause and consider everything you need before pulling it together and sharing it with recruiters.

**Is the purpose clear?**

Someone looking at your portfolio should know within 5 seconds what its purpose is. Are you trying to showcase your skills, capture the interest of companies in a specific industry, or documenting your work?

Everything from how you introduce yourself in your portfolio to the types and presentation of your work will inform others' perspectives of what your portfolio is trying to do for you. If that purpose is muddy or scrambled, it could create the impression that you built your portfolio by scrambling.

**Do you know what key terms you'll use?**

Searching sites like Google Trends or Ahrefs keyword search tool and looking through jobs that interest you, you want to use standard and expected language in your portfolio. Priming yourself by reviewing a few job posts and doing a small amount of keyword research can help inform what and how you share work in your portfolio and what terms you can include in demonstrating your skills or experience best.

**Do you have two or more case studies?**

You will want to convey not only an eye for detail in the work you show in your portfolio, but you'll also want to demonstrate repeatable working habits. Ensure you include the skill keywords mentioned previously organically throughout your case study (and not as a bulleted list at the top). Including a minimum of two case studies in your portfolio is ideal, though you should not have more than six if possible.

**Is your navigation planned out?**

Straightforward navigation is critical to the success of a modern design portfolio. Recruiters and hiring managers often scour dozens or hundreds of portfolios daily. The last thing someone visiting your website wants is not to be able to find and access the things they need to inform their thinking.

Make sure you create a bulleted list or visual map of how a user might navigate your portfolio. It does not need to be a very complex plan, nor do you have to map out a large project. Simple is better, as long as those viewing your portfolio can jump between projects to compare and understand each better.

**Is it going to be accessible and easy to share?**

If you haven't yet considered building your portfolio for accessibility—making sure your portfolio can be accessed and used by as many people as possible—you should do that now. If that sounds like a lot of work, try not to worry. There are two basic tenants of good accessibility design which can help you plan accordingly:

- **Design for the many.** Your portfolio should ideally be responsive: accessible and functional on a large desktop computer and a small handheld phone. You can also consider additional support for screen readers, dark mode, etc. These may not be critical in a portfolio but can often improve the experience of recruiters.
- **Provide clear and consistent information.** Be honest with what you share in your portfolio; consistency will come with it. Also, strive to make your portfolio easy to understand and follow by guiding visitors and simplifying language and writing. (Tools like Grammarly and OpenAI can help with concise writing.)

**Is it clear what you want visitors to do next?**

In most cases, the recruiter or hiring manager is likely viewing your portfolio as part of a review process. They are likely looking at many portfolios, one after the other, to make initial decisions. For these cases, the viewer has a next step already in mind: mark whether or not they are interested in talking with you through their applicant tracking system (or ATS).

But you still have some control and sway on what visitors to your portfolio do next. You can provide large call-to-action buttons throughout your website and messaging about what you hope visitors will do. Examples of primary actions could be:

- Contact me (about a job or for general inquiries).
- Add me on social media so we can connect over job opportunities.
- Learn more about me elsewhere to inform your judgment of my abilities better.

Whatever action you hope people will take (including marking you with a thumb-up in their ATS), you can help drive that action by letting visitors know as much. For example, a simple message saying, *"If you're looking to hire designers who excel at vibrant layouts, get in touch,"* can be surprisingly effective at making your portfolio even more helpful in your job search.

## 16. GETTING NOTICED WHEN APPLYING TO JOBS

When job hunting, the most effective way to get noticed is to build a homogeneous set of materials that represent your skills and that you carefully tailor to the type of job you want. It's best not to overlook the value a little research, effort, and cohesion can have in helping you stand out from the crowd.

In today's job market, where many designers are applying for the same positions and companies are actively searching for designers, having a solid portfolio and résumé is not enough to guarantee hiring teams will notice you. A portfolio of work and a solid résumé are regularly table-stakes. What sets designers apart from others is the work they show through their portfolio and the small details that reinforce their expertise and personal "brand" across materials.

The way to stand out in your job search is to do as many small things as possible to increase the overall likelihood of being noticed and engaged. Here are small ways to ensure your profile gets seen when applying to jobs.

**Research the company and the position.**

If you're going to apply for a job, it's worthwhile to do a small amount of research on them and the position before applying.

While you do not need to spend inordinate amounts of time digging into the company's financials or market size, it is worth looking into things like:

- **Their leadership team.** Who leads the design team (if there is one), and what experience does the current teams have? What backgrounds do they come from that may inform how they think about design?
- **The company's primary offering.** How does the company present itself? Do they have a public mission or principles that could excite or motivate you?
- **The specific need is the company hiring to fulfill.** Is there more information about the role that you can research before

applying? Such as posts from the company's designers or recruiters on LinkedIn or increased competition launching new features.

Before applying, doing a little bit of research to understand the company and the position can give you a better understanding of what the company is looking for and how you can customize your application to fit their needs.

This type of research will help you better tailor your materials and give you a leg up in the interview process if you're able to speak intelligently about the company and the position.

**Create tailored and homogeneous materials.**

Many designers mistake using the same generic application for every job. While you do not need to tailor your résumé or application for every single job, you should consider modifying your application (and résumé, when appropriate) for positions that you are most interested in or believe suit you best.

Recruiters and hiring managers can tell when you've taken the time to customize your materials for their specific company or position. Even a tiny amount of custom messaging will make you appear more qualified and motivated than candidates who submit a generic application and call it a day.

Including a brief cover letter specifically written for the job you are applying to is one step to creating a tailored presentation. You should also ensure how you title yourself on your digital portfolio, résumé, and even social channels, is consistent and aligned with the job title you are looking to get.

Do not, however, go overboard and try to incorporate customization into everything you present to a company. Doing so can have the opposite of the intended effect: making you seem desperate rather than energized.

**Use the exact keywords recruiters use themselves.**

When you use the same keywords recruiters and design hiring managers use, it helps them find your résumé when searching for candidates. It also helps to ensure your résumé is highly relevant to the job.

Use the language you see commonly across job posts and keyword research tools (such as Google Trends) in your résumé, job application, portfolio, and social profiles (if you're inclined). Doing so can signal to others that you have the skills to align with their needs.

**Network with employees at the company.**

If possible, try to reach out to employees at the company you're interested in working for—even if they're not in your immediate network. Employees can't always help job seekers, but odds are they want great designers to join their company just as much as the recruiters since everyone in the company is there to see it grow and succeed. So connecting with employees could be beneficial and not as self-serving as initially thought.

LinkedIn is an excellent tool for this; many employees list their current employer in their profile, so if you have 2nd or 3rd-degree connections at the company (meaning that someone in your network knows someone who works there), reach out and introduce yourself. Let them know you're applying, and if they have any time, you would like to hear their experience working at the company and anything they'd feel comfortable sharing about the open role.

Even if you don't get a chance to get your questions asked by someone at the company directly, simply meeting someone who works there can make it more likely that your name will come up when discussing candidates internally.

Keep in mind that networking is all about building relationships—even if these relationships are only superficial at first—so don't be afraid to put yourself out there when trying to connect with employees of companies before you apply. Worst case, you don't get the job but can still expand your professional network.

## 17. WHEN AND HOW TO WRITE A COVER LETTER

A cover letter is a brief, unique document included with a job application, along with your résumé, explaining your qualifications and interest in the job. When crafted thoughtfully, a cover letter is a great way to introduce yourself to a potential employer, build rapport, and state your intention to apply for a job.

You do not need to write a cover letter for every job you apply to, but if you have done some research and are eager to catch the attention of the recruiting team, a plain, concise, and well-written cover letter can help.

Of course, the task with writing a cover letter is making it unique for each job, rather than writing a template and reusing it for every application on every job. Recruiters and hiring managers can easily tell when a cover letter is being reused, and that can come across as being lazy or uninterested. Better to either build a custom cover letter or not include one (unless required by the job).

### What exactly are cover letters good for?

Your résumé outlines your qualifications and work experience, your portfolio provides detail on your skills, so a cover letter should not try to accomplish either of those things. Instead, a cover letter should be supplementary to your résumé and portfolio: giving you an opportunity to elaborate on your motivations for applying to the specific job, as well as how your skills and experiences may fit the role.

A cover letter is often the first opportunity you have to talk with the hiring team, and if you can briefly explain to them who you are and why you are interested in their specific role, they are more likely to continue investigating your résumé and portfolio of work.

In many cases, a cover letter can make or break your chances of landing an interview.

If you take the time to write a targeted letter tailored to the job you're applying for, it can be a sign that you're very interested in the role, enough to take time to research it and write about why it interests you.

A well-written cover letter can give you a significant advantage over other candidates by demonstrating your motivation and highlighting your most relevant qualifications.

Here are a few tips to keep in mind when writing a cover letter:

- **Start by doing your research**. Find out as much as you can about the company, the position you're applying for, and the team you would be working with. This will help you tailor your letter to the specific organization and role.
- **Keep it short and sweet.** A cover letter should be no more than one page and ideally only a paragraph at most.
- **Avoid repeating your résumé.** Instead, use the cover letter to elaborate on your skills and experience, and explain why you're a good fit for the job.
- **Use strong language.** Use words that demonstrate your confidence in your qualifications and your interest in the specific job. For example, instead of saying *"I think I would be a good fit for this role,"* try *"I am confident that I have the skills and experience necessary to excel in this role."*
- **Be honest and sincere.** The cover letter is your chance to show your personality and give the employer a sense of who you are as a person.
- **Edit carefully.** Make sure your cover letter is free of spelling and grammar errors before sending it off.

## 18. UNDERSTAND THE JOB APPLICATION PROCESS

Applying to jobs can be a stressful, even daunting, experience for anyone. Increasing competition, complex recruiting software, and growing legal mandates have made applying to jobs a frustrating experience for many designers. Understanding why the process of applying to jobs is the way it is can help you make sense of the mess—and turn the process into an advantage.

When you look at the recruiting process from the perspective of a recruiter or hiring team, some seemingly odd steps begint to make sense (and can be seen as even beneficial for you as a job applicant). Here's what you need to know about the modern application process and what it means for you as a job seeker.

**Increasing competition has led to challenges.**

Recruiters and the people they work with are some of the busiest employees inside a company today. There's an ever-growing pool of designers competing for the same job, and companies actively seek out and source candidates. There are regulations and job requirements to manage, dozens of individuals to provide updates to, and dozens of other people waiting for feedback or a reply or a phone call.

Recruiters sort through résumés and portfolios from countless designers every day. They manage communications with candidates and teams at a neck-breaking pace. (Not to mention, most recruiters tend to do multiple open job searches simultaneously.) And they do all this while developing a rich understanding of design and the needs of the company.

The difficult task of balancing the number of candidates applying for a job against determining quality candidates from subpar ones falls on recruiters and hiring managers.

Companies want enough job candidates to increase the odds of finding an optimal designer for a job while simultaneously ensuring thousands of unqualified designers don't apply and create more unnecessary work. Companies use ambiguous job posts and lengthy application forms to weed out candidates who aren't as committed or interested in the job as others and increase the likelihood of getting higher-quality candidates.

**Tools have added complexity for candidates.**

To help recruiters manage their workload, they rely on applicant tracking systems (or ATSes) that help intake, sort, filter, and manage job applications. These systems are great for recruiters but often make it harder for you to get your resume noticed.

Many of these ATSes are programmed to look for specific keywords and rank candidates based on their match to a job description. If your résumé doesn't include the right keywords or doesn't meet the system's criteria, it may receive less attention than other applications.

However, despite the common myth of job applications automatically being rejected by a system or artificial intelligence, the reality is today, a human being still reviews every job application. A recruiter or hiring manager will look through every application to ensure they are not missing anyone. However, recruiters do not treat all applications the same.

Once you submit your application, it goes into the ATS and waits for a human to review it. Sometimes, the recruiter or hiring manager will immediately decide after reviewing an application. Other times they may spend considerable time reading and re-reading an application to signal whether the designer is qualified and well-suited for the job.

Why don't recruiters send a rejection message to you? If you never hear back from a company after applying, odds are your application was received, evaluated, then rejected. Some companies will send a generic message which reads: *"Thank you for applying but we have decided to go with another candidate at this time"* But other companies, the majority of them, will not send any confirmation or rejection whatsoever.

Two reasons companies don't send rejection emails to candidates:

1. **There are too many applications to reject everyone individually.** For companies that deny hundreds of applicants

a day, writing a rejection letter would be incredibly time-consuming and costly.

2. **Candidates waste time arguing.** Even if you don't feel like this applies to you, enough designers actively argue against rejection in hopes it will increase their odds of getting the job. Arguing will not help you get a job (if anything, it will do the opposite), but recruiters can't spend time discussing a rejection with every designer who has applied for a job.

In addition to avoiding arguments from candidates, many companies (particularly in the United States of America) will not communicate about job rejections due to legal concerns. Suppose someone rejected a job candidate for a reason they feel is vital to their identity, for example. In that case, they may sue the business and cause unnecessary (and often unwarranted) legal woes.

**What can you do to increase success?**

Knowing these things, you can take advantage of the situation recruiting teams find themselves in (and the tools they use).

Ensure you calibrate your résumé for the specific job. Use the exact skill words you find in the job post in your résumé. Include a well-written cover letter. And reach out to company members (ideally other designers) to ask for their experiences. Doing these things makes you turn a humdrum process into one that works in your favor.

## 19. THE MOST EFFECTIVE WAYS TO APPLY TO A JOB

With much of the application process being powered by tools and resources that have been built to support companies, designers often feel powerless in the process. You have many options when it comes to applying to jobs and more power to influence the outcome than you may realize.

When applying to a job you first should consider the method of application in order to determine what controls you can play with. A few of the most common ways of applying include:

• On a company's website

• Through a job board, such as Dribbble jobs

• On a job service provider such as LinkedIn

• As a referral, being recommended by a person already at the company

• Through a recruiting or staffing agency such as Creative People

There is no "best" way to apply to a job, and each method comes with it's own set of trade-offs in addition to benefits. Because companies are often eager to get talented designers, any method you choose will be treated similarly as the others. The only exceptions are the latter two options of being referred or going through a staffing agency.

**Being referred to a job.**

Referrals are when someone currently working at a company recommends you for a position. Because the referral is coming from a current employee there's an increased priority for the candidate.

Research has repeatedly shown that designers who are referred to a job convert from an applicant to a hire at a rate of roughly 40%. Referrals also stay at a job longer and report more overall happiness than their counterparts. Is it any wonder why companies love it when they get referrals? (Most companies offer employees a referral bonus in the form of a small gift, or a monetary payment ranging anywhere from a few hundred dollars to thousands.)

Referrals are not guarantees, however, and they are often only as effective as the employee referring you. They also require you to have a close connection with someone at the company who would be willing to refer you.

If you do not know someone at a company, do not reach out to employees and ask them to refer you. Odds are they will ignore you or take offense to your ask, since they don't know you. But if you have a close connection at a company you are applying for, it is highly recommended you apply by first requesting a referral. A few other points to keep in mind about referrals:

- **Make sure you are qualified for the position.** Review the job post, audit your portfolio and experience, and put in the work to understand what the company is looking for from designers. If you are not a good fit, a referral may reflect poorly on the person who referred you.
- **Prepare for your interview as if it were any other.** The fact you were referred does not mean that you do not need to sell yourself to the employer. A referral interview is still a regular interview, though the application (your résumé and portfolio) may receive more immediate attention.
- **Keep in mind that the person who referred you is vouching for your character.** Thank whoever refers you and try not to inundate them with requests for more information or a status update on the job. Asking for feedback from someone who refers you is fine, but they may not have any information to share.

**Working with a recruiting or staffing agency.**

A recruiting or staffing agency is typically a company that will assign one or more people to work with you on your job search. Their role is to understand your career goals, your skills, and ambitions, then work to help find opportunities that align. The recruiting company is often paid by the employer, if the job is filled, so you don't have to pay them.

Not every designer can work with a recruiting agency, as they typically prioritize high-caliber and experienced candidates. Though it doesn't hurt to reach out to one or more of these companies and ask if they can help you in your search. Even if they say no, at least you tried!

The benefits of using a staffing agency include having access to a larger pool of jobs, getting help with your job search, and having someone advocate for you. The company will act as a middle-person to talk with companies, assess opportunities, represent your abilities, and work with you on figuring out which opportunities are more than likely to pan out.

Staffing agencies work with a variety of businesses in different industries. This means that they have access to a larger pool of jobs than you would if you were searching on your own. They can also help you negotiate salary and benefits, and they can provide support if you have any questions or concerns.

**No matter which approach you take…**

The most effective way to apply to a job is to pick one method for applying, try to connect with a current employee or recruiter to understand the company and their needs, and investing in your application materials.

# THREE
# EARLY STAGE INTERVIEWING

## 1. A BRIEF INTRODUCTION TO SCREENER CONVERSATIONS

Your first call with a recruiter or hiring manager is often a screener: a chance for you and the company to determine whether there's a fit for an open job or not. Early conversations like screeners give you and the company a chance to assess what the other offers, build early relationships, and set the stage for what comes next.

Screening—or "screener"—calls are when someone, typically a recruiter or hiring manager, connects with you for the first time to discuss the possibility of an opportunity to work together. These conversations are often conducted over the phone or via video conference and last between 30 minutes to an hour. They're commonly used to help employers narrow down their candidate pool (and to help you narrow down your options as a job candidate too).

Companies often call these calls "screeners" as their purpose is to give both parties a chance to learn about each other and decide if there's value in formally starting an interview process. The call is a chance to "screen" one another before investing more time and energy into the relationship.

Screening calls and other early conversations are only supplementary to more formal interviews. Companies track when first interactions happen with candidates and feedback from the conversations, but screening calls are not formal interviews and should be treated more as an introductory conversation.

Whoever talks to you in a screening call will have considerable sway on whether the process continues. Still, screening calls are not always incorporated into the overall evaluation of a candidate once you pass it and start formal interviews and assessments. Early stage interviews save everyone time by allowing employers to identify which candidates are worth pursuing quickly. These interviews also will enable you to learn more about the company and decide if it's somewhere you'd like to work.

During a screening call, the employer will ask about your experience, skills, and career goals. In these interviews, you'll have an opportunity to provide some information about yourself, and you should use the conversation as an opportunity to ask questions. It's also reasonable in a first conversation to discuss, in brief, the criteria for your career that matter most to you: salary expectations, terms of employment, responsibilities, and career growth opportunities.

Preparing for screening calls by researching the company a bit and preparing questions in advance will ensure the company, and you, get the most value from the time.

In addition to being efficient for companies and designers alike, screening calls can help assess fit, build early relationships with one another, and allow you (as a job candidate) to prepare more thoughtfully for what happens next. You can maximize the value you get from screening calls by asking questions and reflecting on the information you receive.

## 2. HOW TO PREPARE FOR SCREENER CONVERSATIONS

Recruiters may ask you to do a screener call when you first connect with them about a job. While companies do not intend these early conversations to be stressful, preparing for the call can make a difference in how responsive and engaged the company you're interviewing will be.

As you enter the job interview process, you'll inevitably face "screener calls" with a recruiting team member. These 30 to 45-minute informal conversations are great for assessing opportunities and can give you and the company you're interviewing a better sense of whether or not there's a "match." Suppose the interviewer leaves the conversation feeling optimistic about your experience and skills. They'll work with you to schedule more formal interviews later on.

While a screener call may seem like a relatively minor part of the interview process, it's an excellent opportunity to make a positive impression and get your foot in the door. Screener calls are also a perfect way to prepare for the rest of the interview process. You can ask questions to clarify the position, the team, and the job's responsibilities before formally beginning to interview.

Whether you've never done a screener call before or have done hundreds, here are a few tips on how to best prepare for your next screening call.

**Do research on the company and role.**

A small amount of research will not only help you be more prepared for questions about the company, but preparing will also show you're genuinely interested in the opportunity.

Before you hop on a call with a recruiter, take a small amount of time (10 to 30 minutes) to further research the company and the role if you haven't already. Look into the company's mission or vision, founders, the design team (if one exists), and the latest business announcements. You can read and re-read the job description and the company's career page (or LinkedIn page) for more insights into the company.

It would be best if you walked away from your research with a good understanding of the company's purpose, operations, and role.

**Prepare what questions you want to ask.**

It would help if you also came away from your research with questions you can ask to inform your perception of the opportunity. First, assess what information you can find through your research, then compare it to your career goals, ambitions, and experience. Common screener questions you might consider asking include:

- Why is this role open, and what are the expectations? Why now?
- What do the company's core values mean to the interviewer? Can the interviewer share an example of how those values impact trade-offs at the company?
- What have been some of the biggest challenges the team or company has faced recently?
- How is success measured for designers and others at the company?
- Is there a timeline the company is looking to fill the role within? Are there current candidates at later stages of the process?
- Can any compensation numbers or bands be shared?

**Prepare for common questions.**

Many recruiters think of screening calls as a way to "cover the basics" before a candidate moves into more rigorous interviewing with the rest of the team.

As a result, recruiters and their teams commonly ask the same questions you can anticipate before screener calls. These include questions about your experience, qualifications, and motivation in applying for the role.

The interviewer may ask you to talk about your career goals to assess whether what you're looking for in a role aligns with what the company can offer. They might ask you to share an example or two of the type of work you've done, at a high level, to evaluate your experience and articulation of the experience. You can also anticipate early questions about preferences for work location (remote, hybrid, or in-office), compensation expectations, things that went poorly or well in your previous roles, etc.

By preparing answers to these questions in advance, you'll be able to give more thoughtful and detailed responses during the call. It's vital to remember screening calls are screeners: companies don't intend for them to be deep interrogations of your career, so keep your answers as concise and straightforward as possible. Shorter replies are better, and you should feel empowered to end your response with a question such as: "Would you like me to elaborate?"

If you're unsure how to answer a question or how much information to provide, ask the interviewer to clarify what they are trying to assess. Most of the time (though not always), the interviewer will happily elaborate or rephrase their question so you can better answer. Especially during screener calls.

**Be professional.**

Even though a screener call is a relatively informal conversation, it's still important to be professional. Being professional in an interview means avoiding overusing slang, using proper grammar, and maintaining a friendly yet professional tone. Show up on time and treat the interviewer like any other potential co-worker, respectfully but also like a friend you can talk intimately with about your career. If your screener call takes place over video, dress for the occasion as you would for any other interview (and try to tidy your background environment as much as possible).

Screener calls are great for companies and designers to get to know each other. You can present yourself best by putting in a small amount of preparation.

## 3. TALKING WITH RECRUITERS

Recruiters are one of the most underutilized but valuable resources designers have when interviewing. Recruiters are a fundamental part of the hiring team. They have influence and expertise that can help companies find the best person for a role and assist you as a job candidate. If you want to get a leg-up in your interviews, be kind to and build relationships with the recruiter.

Many designers think of conversations with recruiters (or recruiting coordinators or sourcers) as stepping stones to the "real" part of interviewing. Designers will often dismiss recruiters as low-level administrators who oversee the interview process but don't have any sway or influence on the outcome. This is not true.

In reality, recruiters and their teams are core members of the hiring process and are primarily responsible for driving the process to fill a role. When a company offers someone a job, the recruiter gets partial credit for the hire because of their role in the process.

With much of the hiring responsibility falling onto recruiters, they are significant people to get to know and rely on during interviews. Recruiters often have a rich understanding of what the company is looking for and can effectively evaluate designers efficiently because of that knowledge. This means they can also help you: by answering questions, telling you how the process is (or isn't) progressing, and helping coach or prepare you through the entire interview process.

Of course, not every recruiter will be in your corner, nor will they go beyond what's expected in their day-to-day role to accommodate you. However, most recruiters are "people" people; they do what they do because they want to help others succeed in their careers.

Consider being honest with them to get the most out of a relationship with a recruiter. Speak clearly and concisely about your strengths and weaknesses. Treat them as human beings. And do not be afraid to ask them any questions.

**Be honest and upfront.**

When working with recruiters in your job search, you should always strive to be honest and open with them. Not all recruiters are forthcoming, but the vast majority will be just as frank as you are with them.

Remember: *a recruiter wants you to get the job*. If you are a match for the job and end up with an offer, that means the recruiter has done their job well. When you're successful in interviewing, the recruiter is measured as having been successful too. However, they cannot help you if you're partially honest or misleading in your engagements.

If you are afraid to tell the recruiter something, ask them what an excellent way to share the information may be. For example, let the recruiter know if you're shy about discussing compensation. They are there to help you—to a degree.

**Speak clearly and concisely.**

In addition to honesty, it's essential to be clear and to the point with recruiters. Often recruiters are talking to many different candidates at once, so they may not always remember who you are or what you last spoke about together. To accommodate the complexities of their role and get more support for what you need, you can set up each conversation with a reminder or clarification. Such as, *"You may remember last time we spoke, I mentioned X..."* Or *"I want to make sure it's clear, I'm specifically looking for a role doing Y because I have experience doing Z."*

If you have a call scheduled with a recruiter, you can improve how you speak to them by preparing in advance. There is zero shame or embarrassment in preparing for a conversation—recruiters will appreciate it if you come into the discussion with talking points and questions already prepared. Write down any questions or comments and tell them, "I've written down a few things I'd like to cover."

**Be professional and friendly.**

As with any relationship: you get what you give. If you want the recruiter to understand you and how your skills apply to the job, you should also seek to understand their role and what they're evaluating.

Asking a recruiter how their day is going, how the candidate search has been, and what you can do to give them what they're looking for more efficiently are great ways to get the same interest and support in return.

However, it would help if you remained professional in all conversations with the recruiter and anyone else at the company. The recruiter is trying to gauge whether you'd be a good fit, so it's crucial to present yourself in the best light possible while also being friendly and conveying your interest in the company, role, and the recruiter.

**Ask all questions.**

Asking questions shows that you're interested in the position and taking the time to learn more about the company. This is a great way to make a positive impression on a recruiter. It's also an excellent way to calibrate your understanding of the role and the interview process with the recruiter.

If you find you don't have many questions to ask during a call, it's always good to ask: *"What other questions do designers typically ask you?"* Or a fun one might be: *"What question do you find designers typically ask that you wish they wouldn't during these calls?"*

Some of the best and most influential relationships you can invest in during an interview are with the recruiter. You can utilize the recruiter's knowledge of the company and job to inform your perspective. And the recruiter's expertise on how candidates move through the interview process can help you plan and prepare.

By building rapport with them, being honest, preparing for conversations, and treating recruiters as any other critical part of your job search (because they are!), you can get a significant leg up while interviewing.

# 4. QUESTIONS TO ASK IN EARLY INTERVIEWS

Despite how it might seem sometimes, interviewing is a two-sided conversation. As a prospective candidate for a job, it's best to treat the interview process as a way to exemplify your experience and evaluate the opportunity in front of you.

We know that coming up with the "right" questions can feel tricky, and nobody wants to feel like they made a poor impression by asking silly questions or no questions. An effective way to think about what questions to ask in any interview is first to clarify what you need to know about a potential employer.

Most interviewing questions fall into one of four categories, in order of importance:

- Individual (or "fit")
- Role
- Team
- Company

For each question category, you can dig deeper by considering "the five Ws": who, what, where, when, why (and how). For example, when considering the team category, you might ask questions such as:

- Who is on the design team today?
- What are their strengths, and what areas are they lacking?
- Where does the team sit within the business hierarchy?
- When was the team founded, and when was the most recent member added?
- Why does the team exist? What is their primary objective as a group (if they have one)?

Of course, not every question will be equally as valuable to you as they are to someone else. To determine which questions will help you in interviewing, you should evaluate them against your career goals and determine which factors are most important.

Once you have an idea of what questions to ask in early-stage interviews, you can prioritize the questions themselves to accommodate the interviewer's (and your own) time. A prioritized list of questions means you'll be engaged, and the interviewer will feel like you value their time and the opportunity. When you prepare thoughtful questions, you will likely get additional signals and insights that other designers may miss.

That said, I've prepared a set of six questions you might consider asking in addition to any you come up with on your own using the above process.

### 1. Why is this role open, and what specific need did the team identify that makes this role necessary?

When a company opens a role, there is typically a process that defines why the job is necessary. Companies are often careful to determine why a role matters now rather than six months ago or a year from now. If you can understand what led a company to open a position, you can more easily decide if it's right for you *and* present yourself in a way that aligns with the company's needs.

### 2. How does the company evaluate designer performance (or similar roles)?

A vital question to ask in any interview is about performance expectations and how leaders will evaluate the role. If you were to get the job, what would help you succeed? Do you have the skills necessary to succeed, or can you develop them?

Are there timeline and quality expectations around the work? Does the company evaluate criteria such as an ability to communicate or influence others in addition to design outputs? How precisely will performance be considered, and how often will you get feedback on your performance?

### 3. What do you think will be different about this role a year from now?

Best guess or gut reaction, what does the interviewer see as the future of the role? Asking this type of question will often cause the interviewer to pause and reflect, so it's a good idea to give them a chance to think about their answer or to remind them you're only looking to understand expectations and what the company needs.

Asking an interviewer their perception of a role's future can tell you a lot about them, the company, and the position. If a team has given little thought to the role, the company may be fast-paced and "shoot from the hip" in their work. Or they may not understand how this role could evolve. You will have to decide which answer aligns with your expectations for the job and where you're at in your career journey.

### 4. Can you share an example of a time the company faced a difficult challenge?

What was the challenge, and how did the team deal with it? What did leaders do? How were decisions communicated to those outside the decision-making process?

Asking about company challenges can tell you what the company has been facing recently (big or small, financial or organizational, etc.) and also help you better understand how obstacles are passed up or down through the company. Please pay attention to the interviewer's answer as it relates to the communication, collaboration, and responsibility of those involved directly or indirectly with the challenge.

### 5. Can you share an example of how design (or similar functions) decide what to prioritize at the company?

Companies will often talk about their lofty mission and principles, but when it comes to working, those same elements may vanish in the place of other incentives. An excellent way to truly understand what a company's values mean is to ask for examples of how they prioritize their work. You aren't looking for a prioritization process (like what tools the team uses or what framework, such as Asana and agile). What you are looking to evaluate is what values the team has that influence what they work on and how they make trade-offs.

### 6. How is the function of design measured at the company (or how will it be measured)?

Design is not easy to measure, but companies will try many tactics to give it some tangible meaning. Understanding what the company does to measure a function, such as design, can also tell you what role they think the part plays. If they have no measures, that could indicate they are a maturing organization or don't value design as a measurable function.

If you can understand how the role of design is measured (rather than how individual designers are evaluated), you can get to the heart of what the company believes design is for and how it contributes to the larger business objectives.

# 5. AN OVERVIEW OF DESIGN CRITIQUE INTERVIEWS

A standard interview you will likely encounter in the early stages of interviewing with a company is the "design critique." A critique interview allows you to demonstrate your design knowledge while allowing interviewers to observe better and understand how you think about design and feedback.

Critique is a vital part of any design process. Whether you're the first designer at a company or the 1,000th, being able to constructively evaluate a design is a skill that impacts the team(s) you work with within a job. As a result, companies use a faux critique to understand how you think.

The critique interview is a conversation between you and one or more interviewers that seeks to expose how you think about the design of work that is not your own. Commonly, a critique will task you with looking over an existing design—an app, website, brand, or other collateral—and critiquing it in real-time.

**What interviewers are looking for.**

The exact format of a critique interview varies. However, the core of what the company is looking to evaluate through the discussion is the same. So before covering the critique format, it can be valuable to understand what companies are precisely considering through them.

Companies use design critique interviews to understand your strengths in how you think about and evaluate designs. These critiques are an essential part of the interview process because they allow you to showcase your knowledge while allowing interviewers to gauge your ability to think critically about design problems and provide constructive feedback on them.

Interviewers will be looking to understand aspects such as:

- What do you hone in on first about the design you are evaluating? Do you call attention to visuals, the problem the design seeks to solve, customer pains, or something else?

- What values do you place on the attributes of the design? For example, do you comment on the part of the design that follows conventional design heuristics? Do you repeatedly call attention to elements of the design that are unconventional or subpar?
- How do you deliver feedback in real-time? When identifying something critical in the design, do you offer suggestions for improvements or articulate why the original designer may have made the decisions they did?
- Can you identify and speak to use cases other than your own? As a designer, you need to be able to theorize what other people may see and experience from the design and speak to that perspective. Speaking only from your view is not suitable for critiquing a design that was likely not built for you.
- How do you seek to understand the problems the design is solving? Can you vocalize what concerns you think the design aims to solve and how it does or does not achieve what it sets out to do?
- What lens do you take when evaluating designs? Do you think of only negatives, or can you also identify positives? Do you think about the design from the perspective of a team member working on it? Do you talk about how the design might play a role in the more significant business or how the design may be one small piece of a larger ecosystem?

Interviewers will be looking to understand these types of things as you critique.

There is no wrong or right way to do a design critique as part of interviewing, and the best way to ensure you come out on top is to be yourself. Knowing what interviewers will be evaluating can enable you to prepare, but if you critique in a way that attempts to "check all the boxes," you may come across as insincere.

**The format of a design critique interview.**

A critique interview is typically a 30 or 45-minute conversation done face-to-face or over the phone. If done over a video call, the critique will likely entail screen sharing from the interviewer or yourself, so plan accordingly.

There are four critical elements to the critique format:

**1. The selection of material for critique.**

The best interviewers will come prepared with a design for you to evaluate. However, some interviewers may ask you to bring a design yourself or to select from a set of options. In any case, you should not need to prepare for the critique interview. In fact: interviewers prefer not to share a design with you before the interview, so you do not come over-prepared with feedback on the design.

**2. Establishing the critique as a collaboration or evaluation.**

In some cases, the interviewer may not convey whether the critique is collaborative or evaluative. If at all unclear: ask the interviewer their role before you start critiquing. Specifically, you can ask the interviewer if they will be critiquing alongside you or simply listening and evaluating what you say.

If the interviewer is a collaborator, you can ask them questions and help guide them throughout the critique. If they are evaluators, you should focus on driving the analysis entirely at your discretion.

**3. Setting criteria for a successful critique.**

Just as you would an honest critique with a teammate: understanding the context and problem are essential in a critique interview. Before the analysis begins, ensure you are clear on the criteria for a successful critique.

You can get clarity on the critique criteria by asking the interviewer questions such as: "is there anything specific you'd like to focus on today, or any particular part of the design you would like to evaluate?"

**4. The critique.**

When it's time to do the critique, you should dive into the design and focus as much as you can on speaking thoughts aloud.

Because the interviewer will be assessing what you focus on and how you speak to it, there is no universal guidance on how to do the critique. Walk through the app or design as you would a real-world analysis, talking about why you're evaluating a specific part and what your evaluation of the part entails.

An example critique may begin like this:

*"The first thing I'm looking at on this app design is the overall screen. I want to think about what problem this design is trying to solve, and I can see a few things that hint at the problem. There's this large banner at the top of the app that says I can order food at any time, so my immediate response is the app is trying to serve the need of people who are hungry at any time of day or night."*

Continuing with: "I can imagine they put this at the top of the design because they want users to keep coming back to the app. Let's see what happens if I tap on the banner. It doesn't do anything, so that's interesting. It makes me think they could attach an action to it, since it takes up a lot of space. I could see a user who is in a hurry to order food being annoyed by this large banner...."

**Pulling it all together.**

This guide is an overview of design critique exercises, so you should have enough context and insight to feel confident in your ability to critique successfully in an interview.

Ultimately there is no single way to critique, and interviewers do not give a pass or not pass grading. Interviewers want to understand how you think about a design, how you communicate your thoughts, and what type of feedback you might articulate as part of a critique process. If you can do those things, you'll do well.

# 6. GETTING CONTEXT IN CRITIQUE INTERVIEWS

One of the most critical elements of any interview—but particularly for design critique interviews—is establishing context before the interview begins. This way, you and the interviewer(s) can align on what's expected from your brief time together. If you want better critiques when interviewing, remember to set and get context before starting to analyze the design in front of you.

The expectations and evaluation criteria for any interview will vary depending on the company, interviewer, role, and more. Companies strive to ensure consistent and fair interviewing practices (as doing so helps not only the candidate experience but also ensures the company is evaluating designers against the same criteria and, therefore, can assess each individual against the exact expectations).

However, not every company can utilize the same interviewing process for every conversation. Critique interviews are no exception.

As a job candidate, you should seek to approach each interview with a determination to understand what the other person—or persons—in the room are trying to know about you and your abilities.

Establishing a shared context for critique interviews is best to communicate understanding, perception, and expectations. You can do a few key things before you start critiquing or answering questions to establish a shared context.

**Understand the role of the interviewer.**

Some companies train interviewers to conduct critiques and give them considerable opportunities to build their interviewing skills. Other companies may ask interviewers to run a critique with you for the first or second time in their careers. Additionally, some companies view critique interviews as an opportunity to evaluate how a designer thinks independently, while others seek to evaluate collaborative thinking through critique.

To understand what approach your interviewer is taking, you should ask them. It's helpful to start any evaluative interview by asking what the interviewer views their role as.

You don't want to ask the interviewer how they think about their role, implying you're attempting to get an unfair advantage or seek to evaluate them. Instead, you want to set the stage for the interview and clarify that understanding roles is part of that process. Is the interviewer expected to collaborate with you in the exercise or observe? Is the interviewer looking for specific criteria they can share with you? Will they be taking notes or simply listening?

Understanding the role of the interviewer will give you a sense of how to use the time, whether to invite them into the conversation or check in to ensure they understand what you're speaking to or not.

**Align on an ideal outcome.**

Apart from roles, it's good to align on what an ideal outcome looks like for the interviewer. Again, the best way to determine the ideal outcome is to ask.

At the beginning of the interview, ask to align on the ideal outcome. What does a successful interview look like in practice? What would make the time most valuable for the interviewer (and yourself)?

Note the language: an ideal outcome is not necessarily a positive one, nor is it negative. You want to understand what an ideal session is like so that you can operate accordingly and ensure the interviewer gets the information they need to determine your abilities.

**Share your context.**

As you progress through a critique interview, it can be helpful for the interviewer if you talk aloud as you think and evaluate a design. Because the interviewer will want to understand how you critique, it can be beneficial to orient your feedback around your observations and your experience.

Walking through a design will allow an interviewer to note the things you are drawn to or otherwise give attention to, but speaking your thoughts from your vantage can also provide the interviewer insight into your context.

So, if you notice something in a design that feels "off" to you, speak to it and try to frame it from the context of your own experience or expertise. For example: rather than saying something akin to *"This navigation pattern might be problematic, as it doesn't scale as the website grows,"* try instead saying, *"This navigation pattern might be problematic, I've seen from experience how scaling a list-style navigation can lead to a cluttered design."*

Here again, the best thing to do is begin the interview by aligning, saying: *"I am planing to speak aloud as I work through the critique, including some thoughts that may not be fully formed, is that alright?"*

A little time spent setting and getting shared context before beginning a design critique (or any interview) will allow you and the interviewer(s) to align more thoroughly and get the most value from the time.

## 7. HOW TO NAVIGATE CRITIQUE INTERVIEWS

A design critique as part of an interview process is a chance to walk through an existing design and share your interpretation of what makes it successful (or not). To effectively run a critique interview, treat it as you would any review: by setting context, noting what's working and what's not in the design, putting yourself in the role of a real user, and seeking to be constructive in your feedback.

As a design critique or review interview begins, you will want to recall what makes for a compelling critique in the first place. Critique is an opportunity to explore a design with curiosity and an expert eye.

As a job candidate, the critique is an opportunity to share your thinking process when evaluating an existing design. To do that, you should follow a pattern of analysis to spotlight how you assess work.

**First, establish roles.**

Before beginning a critique, it's important to establish roles for anyone in attendance. Your role as part of the interview should be obvious— you are the one doing the critique—but the role of the other person(s) in the room may be less clear. Before beginning your critique, establish a shared understanding of expectations for the other people in the room. Will they be collaborators or provide you with prompts and feedback? Or will they observe?

Additionally, you may ask the interviewer(s) to help you track time and even remind you when you approach the last five to ten minutes of the critique so that you can recap at the end.

**Next, set the context of the design.**

If the interviewer presents you with a design (such as a website, application, or other collateral), you should seek to begin the analysis by setting the context. You can set this context by asking (and providing initial reactions to) questions such as:

- What state is the design in; final and in production, mid-fidelity, or conceptual?

- What aspects of the design should you pay special attention to, if any? Such as visuals, interactions, information hierarchy, motion design, or something else.
- Is there an obvious use case that the design makes apparent? (Here, "use case" means a specific task flow or objective a user or customer might have in the real world when encountering the design.) Is a particular use case that you should evaluate as part of the critique?

If you are already familiar with the design (or if the interviewer asks you to select a website or product for critique), you will want to share your experience with the design upfront before beginning any evaluation.

**Then begin your evaluation.**

Once you and the interviewer(s) establish roles and context, the critique should begin. You can start by speaking aloud about what you observe at first glance. Areas to talk about at the beginning of a critique may include:

- Are there any elements or aspects of the design that stand out to you as good or bad?
- Are there design elements that lend themselves to the (assumed) objective of the design?
- Are there notable elements of the design which are consistent or inconsistent? Are there elements of the design which align with conventional design heuristics (or not)?
- What draws your attention? What is more hidden? Why do you believe each of those elements is the way they are?
- Are there any design elements that business decisions or technical constraints may impact? Are there decisions in the design that you can hypothesize as to why they are the way they are?

**Put yourself in the role of a real customer.**

A compelling critique during an interview will have you "walk through a use case" for the design you are critiquing as if you were a real customer or user. After an initial evaluation of the invention, place yourself into the role of a real user or customer (an ideal, though theoretical, person who might encounter the design in the real world).

Imagine you are a genuine customer, and you are encountering the design for the first time. Then continue your critique by addressing:

- What do you want to do first as a customer?
- What is your objective as a customer, and how does the design help (or not help) you work toward that objective?
- What is confusing as you navigate the design from the customer's perspective? What is readily evident? What might be improved, and if you were a designer working on fixing things, what might you suggest the team do differently?

**Ask questions and share hypotheses.**

Remembering: the point of any interview exercise or challenge—such as a design critique—is to help the interviewer(s) get an idea of how you think about designs. This means there are no right or wrong answers and no "best practices" for navigating the interview. Instead, you should seek to share your thoughts as you explore the design, ask a lot of questions (even if to ask them aloud, left unanswered), and share hypotheses for why the design is the way it is.

If you struggle to speak aloud often, you can ask the interviewer to provide you with prompts. Another method you can try is using a notepad, whiteboard, or similar note-taking system to quickly jot down ideas on one aspect of the design, which you can backtrack and speak aloud about as you progress through the design.

**Conclude with a brief recap.**

As the interview time approaches an end, pause your evaluation and feedback by asking if the interviewer has any questions about anything you have gone over. Then, offer a brief recap of how you feel the critique went. You can provide an insightful summarization by addressing the following items:

- What did you set out to accomplish in the time? (Remember, you and the interviewer should have established this objective before the critique began.)
- How well do you think you achieved the critique's objective?
- What was the context of the design you were evaluating? How did that context inform what you did or did not look at while critiquing?
- What notable design elements consistently drew your attention to them (such as solid brand elements, consistent components, or inconsistent and confusing aspects)?
- What, if any, one recommendation would you give to the team working on the design you just critiqued? Why do you feel that sole recommendation would improve the design?

Finally, conclude the critique by thanking the interviewer for their time. You are unlikely to get feedback on how the critique went, and asking for feedback during the interview is generally disrespectful. Instead, use the recap and end time to reflect on how you believe the critique went. A genuinely successful critique (whether part of an interview process or otherwise) will have the person responsible for the design feel as though they got helpful or valuable feedback from the time.

What would you want to hear from someone evaluating your work? How could their feedback and opinions help you make your designs better? What would make the critique helpful for you if you were in a real-world review and on the other side of the table? If your interview session can provide that type of experience, you will undoubtedly have aced it.

## 8. AN OVERVIEW OF AT-HOME EXERCISES

At-home design exercises are a valuable way for companies to understand how job candidates use their skills and abilities while also allowing designers to showcase their creativity and problem-solving skills.

Design "take-home" or "at-home" exercises are an increasingly popular interview assignment in which a company gives candidates a real-world design problem to solve on their own time. These exercises range from something as simple as redesigning a company's logo to more complex challenges like redesigning an entire website or designing a mobile application from scratch.

Despite their increasing popularity within companies, the general opinion designers have of at-home exercises is overwhelmingly negative. When companies task designers with conducting unpaid work, on their own time, with no guarantee of a beneficial outcome, it is often seen as unfair and inequitable. Nobody wants "homework" while they are looking for a job.

Some designers cannot invest additional time outside typical interviews to work on exercises. People with family or other people to care for, a full-time job (or multiple jobs), etc., are at a disadvantage when it comes to interviewing processes that require work at home.

Still, not all at-home exercises are unpaid, and if you are a designer who can spend time doing unpaid work, it may be worthwhile to manage these interviews.

**Why companies do at-home exercises as part of interviewing.**

There are a few key reasons why design take-home exercises are so important in the interview process. First, they allow employers to see how candidates think through and solve realistic design problems. This valuable information can help employers gauge whether a candidate is a good fit and capable of accomplishing the work that needs to be done as part of the job.

Second, design take-home exercises allow employers to see how candidates handle deadlines and work under pressure. This is important because it can be difficult to replicate those conditions in an interview setting.

Finally, design take-home exercises are an excellent way for candidates to show off their creativity and problem-solving skills. In many cases, the best candidates are those who can think outside the box and come up with unique solutions to challenges.

**Why sharing past work experience is not enough.**

Interviews, like the design process, require making sense of initially incomplete and possibly inaccurate information. A design portfolio may show strong design skills, but it's also relatively easy nowadays for anyone to fabricate a design and create a story to go along with it.

Similarly, conversational interviews can be riddled with designers who misremember information about projects or aren't as great at speaking about their work as they are at demonstrating it. For these reasons, design critiques, whiteboard challenges, and other design exercises can provide companies with vibrant information about a designer they are interviewing.

**What companies look for from at-home exercises.**

Because companies commonly use at-home design exercises to evaluate what a job candidate can do under pressure, in a short amount of time, for a realistic project, they will seek to assess aspects around your approach.

Specifically, the company will want to see the outcome of the exercise and any documentation around the process you used for the project (though it's important to note there is no expectation to follow a specified or "best practice" process!). Screenshots of your documentation, sketches in a notebook, maps and hierarchy lists, explorations, and wireframes are all significant artifacts you can deliver to the company you're interviewing with to help them understand your thinking and process related to the challenge.

The company will seek to understand what you can do with limited information and how to overcome blocks. Do you find a way forward without minimal guidance or get stuck? Can you approach an ambiguous problem with enthusiasm and excitement to do what you do best, or do you shy away from the challenge and view it as more frustrating and stressful than interesting (even fun)?

**What to do when a company requests an at-home exercise.**

If you have the time and ability to do an at-home exercise when a company requests it from you, you are welcome to do it as you see fit. If you are excited by the company and job opportunity, responding positively to the request and conducting it to the fullest of your abilities is best. However, you do not always need to accept the request. Some options you can consider when asked to participate in an at-home exercise include:

- Ask for more time or more direction. Companies are often very receptive to a job candidate's needs (remember: they need you just as much as you need the job). Asking for a few days more time can usually be a reasonable request. However, some companies may limit time as a requirement of the exercise.
- Request an alternative, such as an hour-long collaboration exercise (commonly known as a "white boarding exercise") or another alternative design task that won't demand so much from you.

Companies may view rejection as unfavorable, but you should if you have reasons to decline. However, rather than rejecting the exercise outright, it's best to approach the process with alternatives.

State your enthusiasm for the company and role but decline the exercise for equitable reasons. You can point the company to this article (https://orgdesignfordesignorgs.com/2018/05/15/design-exercises-are-a-bad-interviewing-practice/) from industry veteran Peter Merholz on why take-home exercises are problematic.

## 9. HOW TO MANAGE AT-HOME INTERVIEWING EXERCISES

When you're assigned an at-home design exercise as part of an interviewing process, your success will be determined by your understanding of expectations, managing your time, applying an appropriate process, and using the exercise as an opportunity to demonstrate your skills.

At-home design challenges typically begin with the recruiter or hiring manager providing a prompt and other necessary information. The prompt you receive may be vague or detailed, and it may be either relevant or foreign to your experiences. Prompts for at-home exercises are typically similar to the following:

- Design a mobile application for a pet adoption shelter
- Design a website for a snowboarding company that wants to break into selling skis
- Design an internal set of materials for welcoming new members to a company
- Design a new brand guide book for a global business

These prompts are often intentionally left open and somewhat ambiguous, as the company wants to see what you do as a design candidate to approach problems without much guidance. Regardless of the prompt, the process for what happens next should be consistent.

**1. Ensure you understand what the company expects you to deliver.**

Before beginning any work, you will need to make sure you are completely clear on what the hiring team expects to get from you as deliverables.

It would be best to ask questions and get clarity around what they expect before you begin the work or accept the exercise. Does the company want you to deliver a series of images? Do you need to document your process in written or video format as you work? Will you need to provide artifacts of the exercise via email or a file storage service such as Google Drive?

Ask as many questions as you have before beginning the work, as doing so ensures you can optimize what time you have for the exercise appropriately.

## 2. Set a timeline for your work.

Because at-home exercises are model projects confined to short timeframes (often one to two weeks, at most), it's essential to start the process by evaluating what time you can invest in each stage of the work.

Look at the more extensive timeline and break it down into smaller pieces, such as days and hours. Think about the prompt the recruiter gave you alongside the expectations, then thoughtfully consider how much time you will need to invest to achieve the desired outcome.

If you are familiar with and proficient with part of the design process, you can shorten the time you spend on those areas. Inversely, if there are parts of the process you are not as proficient in, schedule additional time for those.

For example: if the problem space is an area you have no working knowledge of, you will want to give yourself additional time to research and outline findings (such as a full day or two of work). And if you are an expert at building rapid design concepts in a tool like Figma or Illustrator, you can shorten the time you plan on doing that stage of work.

## 3. Plan to apply an appropriate process.

Designers who approach exercises (or any work) by trying to force a process are often unable to work in real-world settings. Problems and projects rarely, if ever, fit into a well-defined process. Attempting to force an approach can lead to wasted time, resources, and poor outcomes. At-home exercises are no different in how you prepare your process for managing them.

You'll need to use an adaptable process that helps you achieve the goal of the exercise in the allotted time. You may not have enough time to do thorough research or explorations. Your final designs may be limited to one or two iterations if any at all. What matters is that you understand what's expected and prioritize your process accordingly.

If you can learn about the problem space through an information list without the need to build a persona or journey map, do not feel like you need to develop a list of personas and related journey maps. Similarly, if you haven't been asked to deliver a prototype of the ideas you come up with, do not feel like that's a required step.

The only requirements for at-home exercises are that you fulfill the request as specified. Everything else is up to you to determine and solve. There should be no pressure to perform a design process that does not accommodate the time and prompt given to you.

**4. Research the space and user/customer.**

In real-world settings, you may or may not have an opportunity to conduct research around a problem by talking to customers or real people who are target users. When it comes to at-home exercises, you likely won't have enough time to conduct research conversations, so you need to get creative with how you develop a perspective of what problems your design will need to solve.

Search online to find relevant studies, social media posts, or articles on the subject area, and use those as references for your understanding of what to design.

For example, say the company asked you to design a mobile application for a small pet adoption shelter. You can search online for things like "What should first-time pet adopters consider when working with a shelter?" to get insights into the pain points and existing solutions the target audience for your designs might have.

Websites like Twitter, LinkedIn, Quora, and Reddit can help you find real-world conversations and questions around the exercise prompt. You can then use these real-world inputs to inform your ideas and solutions.

**5. Aggregate your materials for delivery.**

As you approach the end of your exercise, you should have a myriad of things you can share with the recruiting and hiring manager. Screenshots of notes, sketches, and design concepts are all excellent. Companies will also expect you to deliver your work's "final" result, which may be a set of high-fidelity mockups or something similar.

Plan to deliver each of these materials in an easy-to-understand and explore way. Having a set of folders labeled appropriately can make the recruiter's or hiring manager's job of assessing your work easier. For example: create one folder for "research," another for "concepts," and one for "final designs." Then deliver all of the folders in a single master folder.

**Additional tips for at-home exercises.**

Ultimately, at-home design exercises might sound like work because they are precisely that.

They require tactful strategy and adaptable processes to accomplish a lot of design work in a constricted amount of time. It can be helpful to think of the exercise as an opportunity to do what you excel at and remember the exercise can be a great chance to truly spotlight the skills and abilities you have that set you apart from others.

In addition to everything mentioned previously, keep in mind the following points when doing an at-home exercise as part of interviewing:

- Follow instructions as provided. If you do anything additional or outside the provided instructions, it may create an impression that you are someone who struggles to follow directions.
- Remember to make your designs user-centered. Create a persona or two if that's helpful, and focus on a handful (at most) of use cases that your design will fulfill.
- Simplify the assignment as needed. Delivering a complete set of collateral as instructed is better than giving what you think of as a "perfect" design. You can always include "hypothetical

next steps" as part of your delivery, helping the interviewer(s) understand what you'd do if you had more time.

## 10. DESCRIBING YOUR DESIGN PROCESS

Talking about your design process is not as straightforward as you may think. What interviewers are looking for when they ask about your design process is less about a single, universal way of working and instead about seeking examples of how you approach complicated or ambiguous problems and challenges.

When interviewers ask you to describe your design process, they are not asking to hear about some universal design process you apply to your work. "Tell me about your design process" is shorthand for questions about how you tackle problems, overcome challenges, and approach ambiguity.

Rarely do professional designers follow a singular process; constraints and objectives require designers to adapt their skills and abilities to varying situations. Interviewers often understand that there is no "one size fits all" design process, but they also want to see if you know that and can articulate your understanding clearly.

Questions around the design process ultimately are about the interviewer trying to understand how you approach varying challenges and situations to achieve an outcome. So what should you say if someone asks about your design process during an interview?

**First, share your principles or values.**

The steps and methods you use when designing varies depending on context and constraints, but your values or principles (your "models of design thinking") will remain the same.

So when discussing your design process, you should begin with a summary of your principles (if you have them). For example: if you value inclusive and accessible design, you might say, *"I believe it's important to ensure everything I design is accessible, and you'll see that come out in my process."*

If you do not have personal principles related to how you design, you can speak to your career goals and how those goals play a part in what you work on and how you tackle them.

**Speak about one or more specific experiences.**

Because designers work differently for different projects, giving tangible examples (one or two) of how you have worked through challenges in the past is crucial.

It would help if you came prepared to interviews (and any career conversation) with two or more project stories you can confidently speak to off-hand. These should be personal anecdotes or case studies you can reference to talk about your process, values, challenges, skills, etc.

Be specific and provide details about the steps you took for designing something and be prepared to talk through one or two examples in detail, from start to finish. So, for example, you might begin to talk about your process by saying: *"I can share a few examples that highlights how I like to work."* Then walk through a concise overview of a specific situation you believe that exemplifies your process, from start to finish. Note that your example does not need to touch on every part of a defined design process, nor do you need to share an in-depth look at your process. Instead, talk about what stands out to you in how you work. There will be no wrong or right answers, and you can always finish your example by asking: *"Is there anything more you'd like me to dive into, or would you like me to share additional examples?"*

**Focus on the elements that make your experiences worth talking about.**

Interviewers will want to hear about the parts of your challenging experiences or where you had to do something frightening. The inverse is also true: if there was part of a project or experience that felt unusually easy for you, that could be interesting for the interviewer to hear. If you began your answer by talking about your principles, it's best to speak to examples of work where you lived or applied them.

You don't want to speak about the bland parts of your work experience that won't add detail to how you work through uncommon things. Reciting a popular design framework (such as "double diamond") is not informative for interviewers—you are either too junior to develop your design process or do not fully understand the shorthand question about how you work.

**Examples of note-worthy elements you should speak to when talking about your design process include:**

- Was there a specific part of a project that you found daunting or even debilitating? How did you navigate the complexity? Be as detailed as possible.
- Did you have to learn something new on the job quickly to complete a task? What was it, and how did you go about learning?
- Were there parts of an experience that were stressful for you? What made them that way, and what did you do?
- Have you accomplished things you are extraordinarily proud of in your work? What were the outcomes, and what made you so proud?
- Is there a specific partnership you recall as fundamental for project success? What was the relationship, and how did you contribute?

**Leave room for questions.**

You cannot always know what an interviewer is looking for when they ask you a question about the process, but you can address them in a manner that creates space for additional questions or guidance.

It's always best to clarify that you welcome questions and guidance as you share work experience examples. Saying: *"I'd love to tell you about one project that was really informative for how I explore challenges, but if there's anything I say that you are curious about or that isn't clear, please interrupt me."*

One of the easiest ways to leave space for questions is to make them deliberate and explicit. That is: when talking about your work, pause briefly to drink water or think about what you'll say next. It's natural to think pauses when speaking may come across as you being unprepared or overly nervous. Still, the reality is that pausing when speaking is often interpreted by interviewers as being thoughtful and contemplative (two great attributes for anyone to have).

Suppose you're uncomfortable with making deliberate pauses. In that case, you can prime the interviewer for these pauses by saying something akin to: *"I want to be very clear and deliberate with what I share, and also create space for questions and notes, so I'll take my time as I speak through this with you."*

## 11. DISCUSSING PAST WORK

A common element in almost any interview is discussing your past work. Talking about past work will be a natural part of the interview process, but in some cases, interviewers may ask you to review your past work more formally. In these interviews, you have a chance to speak confidently about your work, give the interviewer insight into your level of experience and ability, and a deeper look at your skills, abilities, behaviors, and habits.

It can help to think of past work reviews as a conversation, where the point of discussion should be the challenges and successes of one or more projects.

Successfully navigating a past work review requires you to be prepared, concise, highlight achievements, and be positive as you discuss the work.

**Be prepared.**

Before the interview, take some time to review your portfolio and familiarize yourself with your past work. Try to think of the work experience itself—what it was like to do the job—as that will help you confidently discuss it during the interview.

Focus specifically on what made your past projects successful. How did you learn or grow in the role? What did you do to help the business or your team? How did your work directly impact customers or users of the design?

**Be concise.**

Try to be concise and to the point when discussing your past work. The interviewer doesn't need to know every detail about your experience. Focus on the central issues alone.

A good starting point for talking about your work is when you first encountered the project, when it was assigned to you or when you brought an idea to the team. Too often, designers get hung up on talking about the minutiae of the company they were working for or the organizational makeup. While those things are essential, an interviewer is not interviewing your past company. They are interviewing *you* and want to hear about you, so talk about your experience, as you recall.

**Highlight your achievements.**

When discussing your past work, be sure to highlight any achievements or successes you achieved. Did you unlock a new feature for users? Did your designs win some award or merit? Did you learn something new or help the business reach a new milestone with your work?

Focusing on your achievements—whatever that means—will show the interviewer that you are a capable and successful designer. Achievements will also help the interviewer understand what you value in your work and career.

**Be positive.**

Always speak positively about your past work, even if the team involved some challenges. In fact: it's best to speak positively, especially about the complicated, complex, or annoying parts of your past work. By showing that you overcame these challenges, you will demonstrate your problem-solving skills and ability to work under pressure.

**End on a positive note.**

Always end your discussion of past work on a positive note, highlighting what you learned from the experience and how it has made you a better designer. Remember, reviewing past work is an opportunity to be critical of what went poorly just as much as what went well. Still, if you end with a positive reflection of the project (such as how it helped you learn a vital new collaboration skill), the interviewer will take away positivity from what you've shared.

## 12. CONFIDENCE IN INTERVIEWING

Confidence is a feeling of certainty about your ability to achieve success. Confidence in interviewing comes down to understanding the process, preparing yourself and materials, and giving yourself what you need to be thoughtful in your engagement with interviewers.

You're not alone if you've ever felt doubt or uncertainty going into an interview. Interviews can feel incredibly challenging. They are regularly high-stakes situations where a company judges your ability to think on the fly, articulate thoughts clearly, and sell yourself as the best candidate for the job. It's no wonder many people get nervous before and during an interview.

The key to being confident in an interview is to be prepared and to use what you know about interviewing to participate in the conversation entirely. If you know what to expect and are mindful of your career story, you will likely be more confident when interviewing. In fact: when you understand what the interview is about and what you have to offer, the interviewing process becomes more like a series of friendly conversations rather than a set of demanding tests.

To increase your confidence in interviewing, consider the following:

**Do your research.**

Before a job interview, take some time to research the company and the role. Explore the company website and social presence on sites like Twitter or LinkedIn. Explore what employees are saying about the company on Glassdoor.com. And consider doing a quick online search for terms such as "[Company name] news" and "[Company name] competitor" to develop an understanding of what the company does and its industry or space.

Investigating some of the company and the team will help you better understand their culture and values and give you a better sense of what they're about and what they might be looking for in candidates.

When you go into a conversation knowing something about the business and those you'll be speaking to, you'll be much more likely to feel at least somewhat relaxed than anxious and uncertain.

**Prepare for common interview questions.**

Specific questions come up again and again in interviews. These include questions about your experiences, strengths, weaknesses, and why you are interested in the role or company. You can practice answering these questions before interviewing to feel more confident about the real thing.

Some of the most fundamental question areas to familiarize yourself with include:

- What design skills are you most familiar with, and have you demonstrated them in the past?
- How do you want to grow as a designer? What skills or areas of development are you looking for in your next job?
- What areas of design are you weakest in and hope to improve?
- How do you work with others, mainly when communicating design aspects to non-designers?
- Why do you believe you would be able to add value to and benefit from working in the role?
- What do you think you may struggle with most if you were to get the role?

**Understand the format of the interview.**

Knowing the company you're interviewing with and the common questions they'll ask is good. Still, you can improve your confidence by knowing what to expect from each interview.

For each interview, you will want to find out whether it will be a panel interview, a one-on-one interview, or something else entirely. You can ask the recruiter or recruiting coordinator what to expect from each interview in advance.

Then, at the beginning of each interview, ask questions to solidify your understanding of what to expect. Knowing what to expect from the interview process will make you less likely to feel caught off guard by any random questions or activities.

Knowing the expectations for each interview and how the interview will likely operate will give you the confidence to maneuver through the conversation.

As a job candidate, it can often feel that you don't have any sway or influence on the interview process. This is not true. Companies want to find talented designers and usually understand that a critical aspect of their search will be helping designers express themselves effectively. To do that, you need to ask for specifics and clarify what interviewers expect during each interview. If you don't ask, you may not know; if you don't know, it's hard to go into the conversation feeling confident.

**Take your time answering questions.**

Slowing down and taking your time can often feel like a waste. When we don't have an immediate response to a question or when we lose our train of thought, it can feel disastrous or like we're leaving the interviewer hanging. The reality is that not everything needs to be said. And the more time we take to be thoughtful when answering interview questions, the more considerate, mindful, and respectful we appear to others.

Slowing down means you're not reacting, and thinking is a significant part of what many companies hire us to do today.

If you need a moment to gather your thoughts before answering a question, don't be afraid to take a brief pause. It's better to take a moment to collect yourself than to rush through an answer and risk getting tongue-tied or saying something that doesn't make sense.

**Ask questions of your own.**

Finally, asking questions shows that you are engaged in the conversation and that you have done your research on the company. Prepare a few questions ahead, so you don't draw a blank when the interviewer asks if you have any questions for them. Aligning questions with your career goals is an excellent approach to identifying worthwhile and valuable questions.

Following these tips can make you feel more confident in your interviews. Remember, the key is to prepare so you can focus on putting your best foot forward and impress the interviewer.

## 13. ASSESSING OPPORTUNITIES EARLY ON

In early conversations with recruiters, hiring managers, and other interviewers, it's crucial to assess the job opportunity against your career goals, skills, interests, and abilities. Evaluating a job against the things that matter to the next step of your career will make it easier to feel confident and increase the likelihood of succeeding in the latter stages of interviewing (as well as on-the-job).

When you have as much information as you can get in the available time while interviewing, determining whether an opportunity is a good fit or not becomes easier. Knowledge also gives you the ability to approach interviewing in the latter stages with focus and intent than if you were to come to those same conversations without sincerely evaluating the job against your criteria.

To assess the job opportunity when talking with an interviewer, you should invoke questions that allow you to build a complete understanding of the job requirements, company culture, growth for the role, and day-to-day expectations. Consider the following when evaluating a job opportunity during early interview conversations.

**Compare job requirements to skills.**

Make sure you understand the job requirements before committing to anything. If you are not qualified for the position, you will either waste time in interviews or get the job only to struggle or have the company let you go later.

The catch is to evaluate the job requirements through conversation and not from something like a job post itself. You also must reasonably understand your skills and ambitions to assess an opportunity effectively. Some questions you can ask interviewers in early conversations to compare job requirements to your skills:

- I see in the job description that [specific skill or requirement] is mentioned. Can you tell me how that shows up in practice on the team today?

- What about my résumé or experience speaks most to you when you look at the requirements for this job?
- I have a personal goal of [specific goal]; how do you see this role helping me achieve that in the coming years?
- When someone does [specific skill or requirement] at the company today, how do they know if they're doing it successfully or not?
- When the company decides to hire or not hire someone for this position, what do you think will be the most critical factor for that decision?

Once you've compared the job requirements to your skills and goals, you can begin to explore the company culture and its implications on the role.

**Dig deep into the company culture.**

A job is only as fulfilling and enriching as the environment that empowers it, so digging deep into the company culture is a must for assessing an opportunity. Your goal is understanding how the company evaluates success and what happens when problems arise.

Company culture is what a group of people repeatedly do without being prompted. To understand a company's culture, while interviewing, you can ask questions about specific instances of how people operate in the business. You might, for example, ask some of the following:

- Can you share a time someone close to your team went above and beyond? What did they do to perform exceedingly well, and how were their contributions recognized?
- When was a recent time someone at the company raised a flag about a possible issue: a customer or business problem? What was the matter, who was the person, and what happened after they raised the concern?
- What happens when someone on the team is struggling? Can you share an example of when someone has struggled and what the team or company did in that situation?

- Can you tell me when someone at the company made a design decision that hurt the business or customers? What was the decision, and how did it impact the business?

**Look to the job's future.**

At their best: a company will write a job post or description to be future-facing and describe in detail what you can expect to be doing in the role. Unfortunately, most job descriptions are present tense, and companies fail to elaborate on how the role may change when you accept a position. This may lead to a surprising experience as you start your new job or lead to a situation where you end up responsible for things you (and the hiring team) never intended.

You can determine what the future holds for the role you're interviewing for (and whether or not that's a future you can see yourself successfully being part of) by asking questions such as these:

- Imagine it's one year from now: what will the person in this role be doing then? How will they have changed the company, in your opinion?
- If the company has hired designers for similar roles in the past, what are they doing now? Have they been able to succeed, and where have they struggled?
- What would success look like for this person in the first 30 days? What about the first 60 days? First 90?
- If this job were to be opened six months from now, what would be different about it and why?

Find out if there are opportunities for you to grow and develop in your career at the company. You may want to look elsewhere if there is no room for advancement.

Take your time to assess these factors before deciding on a potential job. By taking the time to evaluate the opportunity, you can ensure that you make the best career decision.

# FOUR
# LATE STAGE INTERVIEWING

## 1. AN INTRODUCTION TO PORTFOLIO PRESENTATIONS

A portfolio presentation is one of the best opportunities you'll have during the interview process to talk about your work, make a positive impression, and wow interviewers. It's a chance for you to take control of the conversation in a way you don't get to experience elsewhere in the process.

A typical, formal portfolio presentation will be one of the last steps you take when interviewing. At this point, you should have discussed your experience, skills, and ambitions with the company already in some capacity. And you should feel like the job opportunity in front of you is worth investing more time and energy into pursuing.

Even if you're not a confident speaker or someone with a lot of experience speaking to small or medium-sized groups, a portfolio presentation is a lightweight way to help others learn about you, your skills and abilities, and what you're capable of doing as a designer. Knowing what the presentation is for, what to talk about, and how to structure it can make putting together and presenting a few case studies easier than you might imagine. It all starts with understanding how typical portfolio presentations take shape.

**In summary:**

- A portfolio presentation is a 30 to 60-minute presentation
- The audience will primarily be designers but may include non-designers
- Your task is to talk through two or three projects you've worked on
- Making the presentation personal to your career journey is a secret to success
- Your portfolio presentation should be unique and not a rehashed version of your digital portfolio or resume

The average portfolio presentation is a 30 to 60-minute meeting where you will be talking through a prepared delivery of your experiences for a panel of interviewers. The panel will likely consist of designers, a design manager, one or more cross-functional team members (like software engineers or product managers), and occasionally a recruiter or other hiring manager.

Everyone who attends your presentation is there hoping to understand how you work as well as your ability to execute and communicate ideas. The presentation portion of the interview process is substantial because it demonstrates how you show up and convey your thoughts and experiences—it's a real-world test of how you might talk to future coworkers about your ideas or knowledge.

Depending on the role, the interview panel will pay close attention to the core skills required for designers at their company. Meaning: the panelists will want to hear you speak to specific examples of when you had to apply skills in one or more areas, including:

- Visual design and attention to detail
- Interaction design, or how you think about user flows and experience
- How do you consider design in the larger goals of the business
- Your ability to be intentional in decision making
- Your communication style, both methods of communicating in your work and in the presentation itself

If you don't already have one, you need to start building a presentation deck you can use for this part of the interview process.

A presentation deck can take many forms—like a Figma prototype, a Google Slides deck, or my favorite: a deck built with Apple Keynote. Regardless of what format you decide is best for your presentation, it's essential to design a presentation that can work for a panel of interviewers. In other words, you need a deck to accompany your voiceover to tell a compelling story about you and your work.

Unlike a portfolio website or a downloadable PDF of work, a portfolio presentation is a chance for you to control what information is shared and exactly how you present it. While anyone can look at your resume or website and take away what they want, a presentation is a way for you to talk about the work in real-time in a way only you can (for better or worse).

Some companies may request for you to share your portfolio presentation in advance of actually presenting it. Try not to let the request fool you. You should design your presentation deck to be just that: a presentation built for you to deliver.

The number of projects to show in a portfolio presentation will vary depending on your work experience, but it's always best to aim for two or three (at most) projects you can discuss. Showing one large project paired with a smaller project is ideal, as it enables you to demonstrate repeatable skills rather than one-off experiences.

If you're a student and don't have much work to show, that's ok. The portfolio presentation can still be valuable to talk about any design-related experiences you have. If you have a class project, that's fine. Personal projects can be good to show too.

In a portfolio presentation, you discuss your personal experiences with each project. In fact: as you look to picking projects and building your presentation deck, remember that interviewers are there to learn about you. It would help if you did not talk in-depth about your past company or university but your personal experience and journey with each project. How did you feel when the project started, what did you do to collaborate and work with others, and what did you do to navigate the project to its final state (including challenges and mistakes you made along the way)?

The most successful portfolio presentations are the ones that are unique to you and your personal story. Interviewers have to sit through hours of presentations every week, and most presentations are bland. You can make your presentation valuable by focusing on what caused your past experiences to be helpful for you personally. That is, after all, exactly why the interview panel is there.

## 2. PICKING PROJECTS FOR PRESENTING

A typical portfolio presentation will last anywhere from 30 to 60 minutes. With a small percentage of time set aside for questions (both the audience asking questions to you and, just as importantly, you asking them questions), you'll have about 25 to 45 minutes to present projects as part of a portfolio presentation.

Because of the time constraints, talking about two projects is ideal, but if you need to fit more into the presentation, you can speak of three. Using one project in a presentation is fine but might make it difficult for interviewers to believe you have consistent abilities; and it's good to remember the point of interviewing is to show interviewers you have the chops to do the job well.

Interviewers are trying to understand not only how you work but how you work repeatedly. What do you consistently do when faced with a project problem? How do you operate around challenges or roadblocks? How do you pull others into your process and lean on stakeholders for support? If you can talk about two or three projects in a portfolio presentation, you're giving interviewers a chance to understand how you work and how you do so consistently.

So talking about two or three projects is ideal. But when I say "project," what exactly do I mean? A project can be something significant in size and scope, like designing a platform-wide tool from scratch over many months, or it can be a subcomponent of a larger effort, such as creating a single screen to add to an existing application flow or webpage.

A project is really anything that had a definitive start and stopping point for you as a designer. The project can have been completed and changed course of the entire business, or it might have been scrapped due to executive decision making. As long as there's a clear moment in time where the work began and ended for you, it falls squarely into the definition of a design project.

Projects with clear and measurable objectives are best to speak about in a presentation because they not only have a beginning and end, but also a way to measure the outcome. If you don't have measurable work that's ok, your personal measures of success are just as good for the purposes of interviewing.

Remember that what matters when selecting projects for a portfolio presentation is not necessarily how big each project is or how long they took to complete, but rather how they demonstrate your ability to work through different problems.

A good portfolio project to showcase in a presentation will be one that allows you to highlight the things interviewers will be looking to understand about you at this phase of interviewing. They've likely seen your work in some capacity, spoken to you at least a little about your ambitions and goals, and now what remains is to get a look at how you reflect on past work and share your process.

Notably, there are six key areas you need to address through projects in a portfolio presentation:

- **How you work through problems.** Where do you start when a project begins? What do you do if things become complex or uncertain? How do you work with and rely on others for help?
- **How intentional you are in decision-making.** How do you reason about all the various options before making a decision, or are you more of a decide-fast and clean-up later kind of designer?
- **What do you do to operate outside your personal biases.** How do you leverage research, data, and collaboration to inform your decisions? What questions do you ask to get outside your head when working?
- **Your level of relevant skills, in detail.** Do you understand modern design conventions and their importance? Do you have a keen eye for visual information like kerning and nested corner radii? Or are you more "big picture" in your work and instead focus on systems thinking and diagraming user flows?
- **What size and scope of projects have you worked on previously.** Interviewers often want to see a designer's ability to work on large and small problems. Can you design

something small and relatively straightforward as well as large in scope and ambiguous?

- **How do you deliver on objectives.** When you work, do you keep the business objectives in mind in addition to that of the user? How do you help your team keep the most critical things in mind as you work?

Pick projects that allow you to convey examples of your abilities across these areas, and you'll not only impress the interview panel but give them everything they need to make an informed decision about whether or not you're suitable for the job they have open.

Suppose you pick a project that demonstrates your visual skills, but it's a small project that didn't require much exploration or process. In that case, you can pair it with a larger project that may not be as visually strong but was a test of your problem-solving skills and ability to work autonomously.

Pick two or, at most, three projects you are proud of working on. Pick projects you learned something new from or which caused you to stretch yourself. Projects where you faced a hurdle or had to do something new and challenging are the most interesting to share.

If you're struggling to pick projects or aren't sure how to break a more extensive project down into smaller tasks, move on to the following guide in this course. It's focused on thinking about the structure of your presentation, which can give you insight into the projects that will enable you to shine best.

## 3. DEFINING A PRESENTATION STRUCTURE

Once you have an idea for two or three projects you can showcase in your portfolio presentation, it's time to think about the overarching structure of the presentation itself. You can develop an excellent presentation outline quickly with a few simple approaches.

The best presentation tells a strong story, and the most powerful stories in life are the ones that are personal, authentic, and insightful.

When creating a structure for your portfolio presentation, arguably one of the best structures to use is that of a traditional narrative arc of your career. In stories, movies, and practical presentations, an arc goes from setting up the context to an inciting incident through a climax and down to resolution. We call this outline an "arc" because it consistently raises tension in the audience before releasing and lowering it back down. It's this arc that makes a story exciting or worth paying attention to, and it's this same arc that you will use at least three times in your portfolio presentation: once for each of your two projects and once for the overarching production itself.

To structure your portfolio presentation accordingly, I recommend thinking of the arc of your own career story. Your portfolio presentation will be a condensed version of your career, how you got started in design, what projects you encountered that challenged you, and what led you to the moment you are now interviewing.

Think of your overarching presentation structure like this:

- Briefly describe who you are and how you started in the design industry.
- What brought you face-to-face with the first project you'll be talking about
- The narrative arc for project one
- What happened after project one, leading into the second project
- The narrative arc for project two
- What happened at the end of project two

- What both projects have taught you that has brought you to this moment in time

If your career story is interesting, it won't matter how confident you do or don't appear or how well you speak. Chris Anderson, head of the global ideas conference TED and author of the aptly titled book TED Talks, put it best by saying:

> "The only thing that truly matters in speaking is not confidence, stage presence, or smooth talking. It's having something worth saying."

Think about your presentation as a condensed representation of your career, beginning with context on you as a person. Your life experience is unique to you, and others will be interested in hearing about it as it relates to your abilities as a designer. As a result: your story is worth telling.

A good start will warm the audience to how you speak and give them a small amount of context about you. Instead of starting your presentation by making a joke or asking the audience a question, provide the interviewers with a chance to adapt to the presentation by simply sharing candid and personal information about you. What do you do in your free time? What do you love most about design? What are some exciting things you've worked on, or do you have a favorite memory?

From there, you can segue the presentation to landing your previous job or education experience and tail that with how you got to the first project you want to discuss. Think of the presentation as a way to share a rich story about your career journey.

To begin structuring your presentation, try writing down a bulleted list that answers each of the following prompts, in order:

1. What is your name?
2. What are three to six small things you like others to know about you?

3. How did you first get into the design space; was there a specific event or moment in time that made you decide design was what you wanted to do with your life?
4. As quickly as possible, what happened between when you first realized you wanted to be a designer and when you encountered the first project you'll be discussing?
5. What is the first project you'll be sharing? Why are you sharing it?
6. What was the definitive "stopping point" of the first project?
7. What happened between the end of the first project and the beginning of the second project?
8. What is the second project you'll be sharing? Why are you sharing it?
9. What happened between the end of the second project and where you are now, interviewing?

If you can lightly address each of these nine bullets, you'll have a solid outline and structure you can use for building your portfolio presentation. Remember, conveying consistent ability and personal perspective/story is critical.

In the following guide, you'll uncover how to use the narrative story arc to create a fascinating case study for the first and second (and possibly third) projects you discuss in your portfolio presentation.

# 4. DRAFTING CASE STUDIES FOR A PRESENTATION

When you know two or three projects you want to present in a portfolio presentation, it's time to draft a case study specifically for presenting them. You've done most of the work if you already have case studies written for each project as part of a digital portfolio. What remains is to craft a straightforward, concise, and personal story you can present in a way that gives interviewers a vivid picture of how you have historically made decisions and navigated work.

Presenting design projects in person will be similar to the format used for creating a digital work record. A case study—an in-depth and personal story of what happened and why—is the optimal format, as it highlights the specific details of your experience with each project.

The interviewer or interviewers you present to will want to understand your problem-solving abilities and the impact or results of your work. It's best to tell the story of you and your experience. Similar to a written case study, an effective way to begin outlining your case studies is to tell a compelling narrative. But for presenting, you will want to focus on high-level milestones of your story rather than creating a detailed outline at the start.

So, to begin drafting your presentation case study, take any existing case study or start anew by outlining the following six milestones for each project. A simple bulleted list written in a text document or similar tool will suffice for your draft.

- **Begin with a set-up:** How did you learn about the project? Skip the unnecessary and often cluttered context of the business or industry and start your story with where it began for you. Did someone assign the task to you, or did you devise the idea with a team member? How did you understand the problem, and why did this project matter to you and the business?
- **Move to rising action:** What did you do first when you heard about the project? Did you find a way to talk with people more knowledgeable about the subject? Did you create a list of

known knowns and questions? What were you afraid of, anxious about, or excited to tackle at the beginning of the project? What did you do to explore the work? What were some of the challenges you faced while working?

- **Then the story climax:** What did the work look like in its peak state? When did you and the team know you had landed on something valuable? Was there a specific moment in the project that made you go "aha"? How many iterations did it take to get to the project's climax?
- **Success or failure:** What happened after the work reached its peak? Did the team launch the work, or did it get stuck in limbo? How did that make you feel like a contributor or owner of the project?
- **Falling action:** Reflecting on the state of the work once you began wrapping it up, what did you learn? Were there things you realized you (and the team) could have done differently or better?
- Finally, **resolution:** In one slide or less, where is the project today? When you think about the project, what stands out about your experience working on it?

By following this format, your case studies will be authentic and exemplify what interviewers want to hear: what you did in a specific context and what happened as a result. And the bulleted list you have created will serve as the overarching set of slides you will make when you design your presentation deck. In other words: each bullet you create in your case study outline will translate to a single slide in your presentation.

Once you have outlined each milestone, fill in the details by adding sub-bullets or lines to each section. Your objective with the additional bullets is to highlight specific information that clarifies the parent bullet point or subject area.

For example: if your third bullet point around "rising action" says, "This was my first time in the problem space so I needed to do research to understand the market," your sub-bullets may entail items such as:

"conducting a competitor analysis" or "creating a map of all the elements in the problem space."

When designing your presentation deck, you will want one to two slides per bullet point in your draft case study. Each slide will focus on visuals of the bullet point: so showing rather than presenting a wall of text.

**Additional tips for drafting your case study**

To get the most value from the time you spend presenting your work in an interview, you will want to ensure two things come from your case study drafts:

**1. Get ahead of questions or concerns.**

If there is an element or question you think interviewers will have around your case study, it's best to get ahead of it. By calling attention to a concern or asking yourself a question you think you may get asked in the interview, you can not only appease the interviewers but also show them how thoughtful you are around your communication.

**2. Let the work shine visually.**

The difference between a written case study and one you present is that you do not need to convey as much detail in your outline with the presentation format. Because you will be there to speak to the story you're telling, your outline can be focused on high-level signals and leave the details to your speaking. A good rule of thumb you can use when preparing any presentation is: if in doubt, leave it out.

Because your portfolio presentation will be a presentation—with you there to speak about the work—the interviewers will have an opportunity to engage you with questions about anything you don't include. Interviewers won't have time to listen to every possible detail about your project. Better to index by excluding potentially unnecessary information to which you can later speak rather than cramming them all into the limited amount of time you'll have to present your work.

# 5. DESIGNING YOUR PRESENTATION DECK

With your structure and case study outlines prepared, all that remains is to design the deck and bring all the pieces of your portfolio presentation together. What makes a portfolio presentation valuable for both you and the interviewers is that it gives both parties a chance to see and hear about you and your work. By focusing on solid and clear visuals for your story, you add clarity to what otherwise might be vague or ambiguous in the stories you tell about your experiences.

If you have not yet created a structure and outline for the case studies you'll be presenting in a portfolio presentation, don't worry about how to design your deck. Instead, go back and figure out what projects you'll explain, the structure for the overall presentation, and draft the outline for the projects you'll be presenting before you think about how to design your deck.

Designing your presentation deck should be about creating simple, visual slides for each of the major talking points of your case studies while expressing your experiences and personality in the mix.

There is no minimum or a maximum number of slides to use in a portfolio presentation. Still, it can be helpful to consider your slides as bookmarks in the story you're telling: reminders to yourself about what you want to talk about and emphasize for the audience. Too few slides, and you may find yourself lost or confused (and your audience will be too). Too many slides and you may equally confuse your audience or overwhelm them. The right amount for you will be personal to your story and way of speaking.

Additionally, you can use fewer slides to help draw attention to what you're saying: since slides won't often change, interviewers will be more inclined to look and pay attention directly to you. In contrast, using many slides can increase excitement and energy in your presentation as the material shifts every few seconds.

The "right" amount of slides for your presentation will depend on the structure you've outlined and the key points of your story you should have already outlined for your case studies. Each key point of your personal experience in the case study can stand as a slide. Additional slides will be strictly visual: anything that highlights specific details in your designs or explorations.

An effective presentation will use slides to enforce or emphasize what you're saying. A presentation is, after all, designed to be presented, not something you share with someone for them to go through and understand independently. To design your deck effectively, you can rely on a few time-tested principles for what makes a presentation valuable:

- **Use slides to reinforce your words.** Presentation slides will strengthen what you're saying, give it soundness and help the audience understand and pay attention. When discussing research or how you explored different design concepts, show photos of you talking with customers or screenshots of your messy Figma files.
- **Use large, full-screen images where possible.** Whether you're presenting in real life from your laptop screen or remotely over a Zoom or Google call, people will want to see the details in what you present. Try to use large, full-screen imagery when possible. Get rid of page headers and "chrome" (what is commonly refered to as the outline of a laptop or phone around your designs) and instead show your designs bare. If you talk about a specific part of the design, add a slide that zooms in on that part rather than highlighting it in another way. If you're talking about research or collaboration, show a giant photo of the research or collaboration in action. You can never make an image too large when presenting, and if you feel you need to show multiple images, consider using numerous slides with one image per slide instead.
- **Avoid using text.** If people are reading what's on a slide, they are not listening to you. If they're not listening to you, you lose control of what they are thinking about and how they interpret what you share. The only times you should use text on a slide is if you can make it enormous or when there is no better visualization for what it is you're saying. Otherwise, if you feel

compelled to use text on a slide, plan to read the slide aloud with the audience by saying something like: *"I'll read this with you, so we're all on the same page."*

- **Conversely, use text to emphasize specific points.** If you want to enforce an idea such as a number (say, a "42% increase" in customer feedback) or to include a quote in your deck, text may be appropriate. Big, large text exemplifies a point where imagery may be unable to.
- **Do not use transitions.** Slide transitions can be fun but often detract from the overarching presentation. The only time you should consider using a transition is when it adds something to the story. Having elements of a design fade in over one another can convey how an idea evolved, for example.
- **Focus on the work you're presenting.** To add your personality, emphasize your story, and make your presentation compelling, focus on showing your work. Giant, full-screen slides of your explorations and design details are what hiring managers want to see in a portfolio presentation deck. Anything else is either nice to have or unnecessarily complicating the presentation.

The best summarization of what makes for a good presentation slide comes from Seth Godin, a famous marketing guru, and author who said:

> *"The home run is easy to describe: You put up a slide. It triggers an emotional reaction in the audience. They sit up and want to know what you're going to say that fits in with that image. Then, if you do it right, every time they think of what you said, they'll see the image (and vice versa)."*

# 6. BRINGING A PORTFOLIO PRESENTATION TOGETHER

A portfolio presentation does not need to take a lot of time to prepare. You will impress interviewers if you create a presentation that focuses on your personal story and experiences working with others to accomplish your efforts. But you can only make a comprehensive portfolio presentation once the core pieces are ready and you know what tool you'll use to bring everything together.

The fundamental pieces of a compelling portfolio presentation are:

- Two or three projects that exemplify your experiences and strengths
- A clear, narrative-based structure
- A comprehensive collection of large, representative images
- Confidence in the outlines of your case studies
- And confidence in yourself, of course

Once you've got the pieces ready, you can move to bring them together in your presentation deck. The software you use for your presentation does not matter too much. However, the software you use to build your presentation must be accessible with or without internet access. It's also best to create your presentation in a way that's easy to share with others in case you need to have someone else present it while you speak. Most critically—ensure whatever tool you use allows you to control the timing of the presentation.

For these reasons, it is typically best not to use a static PDF or a website to create your portfolio presentation. Some of the most optimal tools you can use for creating a portfolio presentation today are:

- Figma (by using simple prototyping flows)
- Apple Keynote
- Microsoft PowerPoint
- Pitch.com

Note: if you create your presentation using an offline tool (such as Keynote or PowerPoint), hosting it on a cloud service provider is best.

Using Google Drive or Box to store your completed presentation ensures you can access the presentation from anywhere (if needed).

When you've got all the parts of your presentation together and know what software to use, start building your presentation by creating a blank slide for each key point in your structure/outline. Begin with a single slide with your name in large type (so the interviewers know who you are). Follow the name slide with one or two talking about who you are as a person and designer. Then slides for your first case study, followed by your second case study. Finally, a "thank you for your time" slide with your name again at the end.

Once you create the initial outline in your presentation tool, you can add presenter notes around what you want the slide to present and begin adding images. Remember to use slides to reinforce your words (not in place of them). Add your pictures and remember to run through the presentation as you create it to ensure the story you're telling is clear, comprehensive, and easy to follow.

Lastly, here are a few additional tips to help you pull your presentation together:

- **Help the audience empathize.** Instead of using a persona to describe your work, invite the audience to take the persona's place. Say things like: *"As you can imagine, this is a difficult situation…"* or *"Imagine you wanted to wow an investor…."*
- **Don't try to memorize your script word-for-word.** Give yourself opportunities to tell the story as you recall it, naturally. Not only will your account be easier to remember (it happened to you, after all) it will also come across as much more unique and exciting.
- **Create space for detours.** You can never fully know what interviewers want to hear or see during an interview, so it's best to design your presentation in a way that allows for "detours" in the conversation. Embedding time for the audience to ask questions throughout the presentation is good. Even if they don't have questions, it can come across as thoughtful and like the presentation is a conversation.

- **Do not read your presentation.** If you use text on the screen as your script or rely heavily on notes on the screen to remember what you want to say, you'll lose the interviewers' interest. Instead, embrace the opportunity to talk about your experiences and remind yourself that if you forget to say something: nobody will know but you.

# 7. ADDITIONAL TIPS FOR A PORTFOLIO PRESENTATION

Presenting can always be stressful, and a portfolio presentation as part of interviewing is no exception. To impress interviewers with your presentation, you should come prepared, practice being calm and taking your time when speaking, focus on your story as a designer and how you like to work with others, and be ready to elaborate on your design thinking and decisions.

Despite the term "presentation" being in the title of this interview step, when presenting a portfolio of work, it's best to think of the time as a conversation about yourself. Interviewers will be eager to hear who you are, how you work through problems and challenges, and to see some of the work you've prepared.

**Prepare by rehearsing, not memorizing, your presentation.**

To be clear, concise, and informative when presenting your portfolio deck, you'll want to prepare before the interview (but not too much). If you come underprepared, it will be apparent to interviewers that you are making things up as you go and stumbling through your presentation. But if you come over prepared, you may unnecessarily stress yourself out about specific talking points.

The best way to present effectively is to rehearse your presentation numerous times before your interview. Your objective should not be to memorize the presentation but to be comfortable talking through the primary points and images you have compiled. If you forget a talking point or an interviewer asks you a question that takes your narrative in a different direction than what you had planned, that should be ok!

**Make the interview about who you are, not who you want to be.**

It's easy to put on a faux version of who we want to be when presenting ourselves. After all, we want to show the best parts of ourselves and not any mistakes or struggles we've had. But by not being authentic to who you are as a designer, you may face challenges in the interview or, later on, in additional interview stages, or even if you were to get the job.

Interviewers want to hear you reflect on yourself, your experiences, ambitions, struggles, triumphs, strengths, and weaknesses. Part of authentically presenting yourself is to speak openly about these things. If you feel comfortable doing so: tell the interviewers when you're nervous or excited. Ask if they have questions or if anything is unclear.

The only subject areas you should avoid are: being overly critical of yourself or those you've worked with in the past, not seeing any positive outcomes from past work experiences, or seeking validation as part of the interview itself (for example, by asking: "Do you think this is a good presentation?" or "Do you think I have what it takes to get this job?").

**Treat the presentation as a conversation.**

It would help if you freely asked the interviewer or interviewer questions as you present and invited them into the story you're telling. Though you may not always get a receptive audience, interviewers want to feel like you're not merely talking at them in your presentation.

Invite interviewers to imagine themselves in your shoes while you talk through a challenge you had. Or ask them what they would have done if they were designing something you have done, then surprise them when you did something unexpected or acknowledge your similarities when you mention you did the obvious thing.

Finally, as with any presentation, remember to thank the interviewers for their time. They likely do many interviews every day or week and often see designers repeatedly sharing the same mundane presentation. You'll undoubtedly wow the interviewers by sharing your unique story and perspective on your past experiences, speaking confidently about your journey, interviewing about who you are, and treating the presentation as a conversation.

# 8. AN INTRODUCTION TO PROBLEM SOLVING (AND WHITEBOARDING) EXERCISES

Problem solving exercises can be intimidating and frustrating, but they allow you to demonstrate your problem-solving abilities. And they enable companies to evaluate how you work in real-time instead of reflecting on past work experiences.

One of the final design exercises you will likely encounter while interviewing is what's known as a problem solving exercise or "whiteboard design challenge." Typically these types of activities take place during a "batch day" (also referred to as "onsite loop") and entail you working with one or more interviewers to explore a problem space together.

These exercises often entail sitting in a room—virtually or in real life—and being given a prompt for a problem to solve. The interviewer or interviewers will then ask you to explore the problem alone or as a collaborator. Example prompts you might see in a problem solving exercise include:

- Design a new type of calendar app
- Design a refreshed brand for an outdated company
- Explore how a company can add a unique offering to their existing website
- Design a new interface for a car without a steering wheel
- Figure out how a small city can design a solution to help with crowded parking downtown

Companies often utilize problem solving exercises to allow designers to demonstrate their skills and thinking in real time. Whereas other parts of interviewing are retrospective or hypothetical, a problem solving exercise will enable you to show off how you approach and think through design problems.

Problem solving exercises are an effective way for interviewers to get a signal on skills that aren't always evident in a portfolio or résumé:

problem-solving ability, product thinking and scope analysis, communication, collaboration, prioritization, and more.

Through problem solving exercises, companies will seek to evaluate your problem-solving ability. Specifically, interviewers will be looking for specific behaviors during these challenges:

- Do you shy away from an ambiguous or daunting task, or are you the type to dive right into a problem?
- Do you jump to conclusions or ask a lot of questions?
- How thorough are you when exploring a problem or potential solution?
- Do you ask to clarify the objectives of the challenge and what the outcome might be, or make assumptions?
- Do you suggest the most straightforward solution or try and push boundaries?
- Do you doodle when you think or write or openly talk it through?
- Can you effectively manage your time?
- Can you lead a conversation?
- Where do you ask for help?
- How do you take direction?

Your approach to tackling design challenges will be mostly unique to you. However, there are universal steps to solving problems that you'll probably be familiar with in your experience. First, identify everything you know, then find a way to figure out what you don't yet know.

If you feel anxious or uncertain going into a problem solving exercise, note that those feelings are entirely valid. However, the point of the interview is not to test your ability to solve the problem presented to you perfectly. Instead: the interviewer(s) want to see what you do with your feelings. Suppose you can press through the fear or uncertainty to start making sense of the problem presented to you. In that case, that will get you moving on the challenge while also giving the interviewer(s) a signal on what they need to assess your problem-solving abilities.

## 9. HOW TO NAVIGATE PROBLEM SOLVING EXERCISES

Problem solving exercises or design challenges task you with tackling a design problem that is likely to be vague and ambiguous. You can demonstrate your problem-solving abilities while impressing any interviewer by getting clarity on expectations, identifying what's obvious, exploring unknowns, and saving time for reflection.

Suppose the purpose of problem solving exercises is to give interviewers a chance to evaluate your problem-solving abilities. In that case, navigating these interviews is done by getting aligned on expectations, managing your time, exploring freely, and leaning into your strengths as a design thinker.

**Before you begin the exercise.**

As with most any design challenge in interviewing, it's critical to get clarity on the expectations of the interview. Before you begin ideating solutions, talk with the interviewer about what they expect from you:

- Is the interviewer looking for any behaviors or skills in particular?
- Will the interviewer act as a collaborator you can lean on for creativity and guidance, or are they solely there to monitor you?
- Are you expected to end with a single solution, or is it enough to land on one or two rough ideas?
- Will the interviewer help you keep track of your time, or do you need to set a timer for yourself?
- Should you plan to solve the problem somehow or work through it as best you can?

Typically for problem solving exercises, you'll have access to writing tools like sticky notes and paper or a whiteboard—or, if participating in the activity virtually, a Figma or Miro board or similar virtual canvas. If possible: write down the agreed-upon outcome in big letters on the whiteboard or digital canvas so you can remind yourself of it throughout the exercise.

You can develop a bullet list of expectations and high-level stages for the challenge. For example: define, understand, brainstorm, iterate and test, and reflect.

**Start by identifying what's obvious.**

Once you are comfortable with the expectations for the time, you should capture everything obvious or known to you around the prompt. There is no right or wrong way to begin solving the problem, but by writing down what you know for sure, you can further align on the exercise.

If the interviewer is playing a collaborative role, ask them what you can be sure of and what you'll have to assume. Is the problem apparent, or does the problem itself need to be clarified? For example, if your exercise prompt is about designing a new feature area for an existing website, you'll want to determine who has the problem and why it is an issue for them.

Additionally, consider exploring aspects such as:

- What are the constraints of the problem space? Should you invest time defining additional ones before diving into possible solutions?
- What type of person or customer matters most in the scenario, and who matters least?
- What are the business objectives in the scenario?
- What hurdles might you be able to predict right away?
- If the problem is realistic, ask if the team has already tackled it before. If so: are there any learnings the interviewer can share from their efforts?

Write down everything you or the interviewer(s) ask, along with any answers or possible answers as they arise. Draw these questions and ideas if that's how you think best. A little less than half the time you spend on the problem solving exercise should be asking questions, writing down assumptions, and aligning definitions/goals with the other person in the room.

You want to develop as clear an understanding as possible about what the problem is you're attempting to solve, why it's a problem, and what you might be able to do to resolve it.

Once you've asked as many questions as possible and gotten as many answers as possible, you're ready to ideate.

**Explore what's unknown.**

When you have a clear list of things you know about the problem space, you can begin exploring what you don't know. By connecting known aspects and open questions, ideas should start to make themselves apparent to you and the interviewer(s).

Focus on diverging ideas first by exploring the extreme ends of the landscape you defined in the previous stage: go as far into one possible solution as possible, then jump to the other end of the spectrum and do the opposite. Repeat until you formulate a more realistic vision of a viable solution.

- If you know the problem primarily affects a specific type of person, what does their "user journey" look like, and how can a digital product influence that experience?
- Are any existing solutions you can reference for guidance?
- What might possible new solutions look like, or how might they behave?
- Where might new solutions fail, and where will they succeed?
- What trade-offs will you have to consider while working toward a solution?
- What edge cases can you think of arising?
- What tools or resources might you leverage in building out solutions?
- How does technology play a role in the problem you're exploring, and what facets of digital tools can help create a solution to the problem?

During the ideation stage, it's good to bring in the interviewer again if they are playing a collaborative role and not merely there to observe. Make the activity into a brainstorm and utilize the interviewer for feedback, for coming up with ideas, or for flagging things you might have missed (it's ok to say: *"What am I overlooking?"* and *"Does this feel like a good direction to you?"*).

Always tie what you're doing back to the expected outcome and the problem you're solving.

After a reasonable amount of time, you'll want to start converging on ideas, looking at the most feasible solutions or the ideas that get you as close as possible to the expected goal. Start narrowing down some of your explorations and explain why you're doing so: *"Concept A is strong in this area, and concept B is strong in this other place. I want to briefly explore what would happen if we focused on the best traits of each as a single possible solution."*

**Save time for self-reflection.**

When there are about five minutes left in the interview, it's good to stop and reflect on where you've ended up and the process you took to get there. You will want to speak aloud about questions such as:

- Did you solve the problem or prompt? Why or why not?
- Are you happy with where you ended up or dissatisfied?
- What would you change in your process or approach for next time?
- What surprised you about your approach, and what felt normal?

Interviewers want to see self-awareness and reflection, as both are essential traits of a good problem solver.

**Additional tips for mastering problem solving exercises**

To maximize the time you have in a problem solving exercise, you will want to consider the following tips:

- **Speak your thoughts aloud.** Interviewers cannot read your mind, nor will they always ask questions about your decisions, ideas, or process. It's best to speak aloud as you work through thoughts and brainstorm. If you're not used to speaking aloud as you work, practice doing so with a friend or collaborator before your interview. You can also use written language as a signal during the interview, writing down your thinking instead of speaking it aloud.

- **Get to a "handoff" state as quickly as possible.** A good rule of thumb to keep in mind with a problem solving exercise is this: how can you get to a "handoff" deliverable as quickly as possible? In other words, work through the exercise interview as soon as possible while thinking of your notes and drawings as something you might deliver to a collaborator. Will your scribbles and notes make sense to someone not in the room? If you provide your ideas to someone else, will they know what to do with them? If you can ensure your exercise leads to some "handoff" like the result, you will be communicating and conveying ideas vividly.

- **Note constraints and trade-offs of your decisions.** One of the most vital elements you convey in a problem solving exercise is how you decide what you'll do next. If there's a constraint you are unfamiliar with or a trade-off you want to make quick, voice your rationale and move on.

- **Manage your time ruthlessly.** Due to the short time, you must be decisive in approaching the problem and solution ideas. Embrace skipping steps you wouldn't get otherwise in a real-world scenario. Saying, "For this exercise I'll not do X," can help interviewers understand your thinking while also ensuring they recognize you are making a deliberate trade-off due to time. This exemplifies awareness of the situation and strong decision-making as part of the interview.

## 10. WHAT ARE USER RESEARCH EXERCISES?

User research exercises—as part of a job interview—place you into a simulated conversation to assess how you glean insights from what's said. If you are unfamiliar with conversational research techniques, such interviews can be intimidating. By focusing on the conversation itself and the key points or themes you hear, you can ensure the interviewers get the positive signal they need.

What is a "user research exercise?" In these conversations, interviewers seek to understand how well you listen and engage with mock customers by putting you through a simulated research conversation. Interviewers will look to evaluate what details you pay attention to and how you glean insights from what you hear, then how well you synthesize and share those insights back to someone. These interview exercises can take shape in various formats but ultimately seek to evaluate how you conduct, evaluate, and share user feedback—a core skillset for any designer to have.

In the real world, teams may expect designers (and others across a team) to conduct some amount of research and synthesis, particularly at smaller or early-stage companies. Companies consider user research exercises to be helpful mechanisms for assessing how candidates approach such conversations.

Specifically, interviewers will be evaluating things such as:

- How well do you listen?
- How well can you ask questions relevant to the customer and their context?
- What insights do you pick up through a conversation with a customer?
- Do you take the customer's pain points at face value or dig deeper into what the customer is experiencing?
- What do you do when a customer delivers feedback that disagrees with your perspective or understanding?
- How well do you synthesize and share back customer pain points?

Because research exercises can take many shapes, it can be challenging to know how to maneuver through them. If you are well-prepared for customer conversations, it won't matter what form the research exercise takes because you will have the skills necessary to navigate the conversation effectively. Still, if you haven't had an opportunity to do much customer research in your career, research exercises can feel intimidating and, at times, confusing. Approaching each conversation of a user research exercise as a chance for you to learn about someone else and their thinking—their issues, perspectives, and ideas—and you will set yourself up for success.

An interviewer may moderate a research exercise and act as a collaborator, or it may go unmoderated and you will be the sole "research" participant in the conversation. The interview may involve a single person who role-plays multiple people throughout the exercise or it may involve two or more people who play different roles (once role being that of a customer and the other a team member you will share learnings with). It could be a single or multi-step interview that takes as little as 30 minutes or as long as two hours. As with any exercise or interview conversation, it's important to get context up-front before the exercise begins. Once underway, your job will be to listen intently and naturally curious about what's shared.

You will most likely be allowed to take notes (on your laptop, phone, or with pen and paper) and want only to capture the unique aspects of what you hear throughout the exercise—as opposed to everything word for word. Jotting down key phrases or words will enable you to reflect back on the conversation, and repeating what you hear the mock customer say (in your own words) will ensure you're synthesizing their pain points correctly.

Similar to other interview exercises: the objective is not to complete the research assignment thoroughly with incredible depth to what insights you glean. Instead, the purpose is to give the interviewer(s) a glimpse into how you might conduct yourself in a real-world setting.

Focusing on being a keen listener, documenting and synthesizing (or making sense) what you hear, and communicating what's exciting or most frustrating for the simulated customer will inevitably give the interviewer the signal they need.

If you are unfamiliar with user research and want to brush-up on your research skills before an interview, I recommend browsing the website dscout.com for learning the ins-and-outs of research practices.

## 11. GETTING CONTEXT IN USER RESEARCH EXERCISES

User research exercises task you, as a job candidate, sitting through a simulated research conversation with one or more interviewers posing as customers and team members. As with any problem-solving interview: to come out on top and demonstrate your abilities to the best of your ability, it would be best to begin the exercise conversation by setting and getting context on the interview AND the simulated world you'll be playing within.

Unlike other interviews, the user research exercise will require you to get context twice.

The first context you'll need to establish is on the interview itself: what do the interviewers expect of you, what does an optimal outcome look like, how much time should you dedicate to the exercise before reflecting, and what will the roles be throughout? Once the simulated conversation begins, you will need additional context on the customer and their problem(s).

Because there will be limited time to get to a place where you are demonstrating value for the interview, you will need to move quickly and efficiently through the conversation. It's best to optimize what you'll say and focus on first establishing context for the interview itself. Even if you already know what the interviewers expect, it can only help you (and the interviewers) ensure context is shared and clearly understood.

Ask—and, if possible, write down—what the expectations and optimal outcomes are for the interview. You will want to ensure both you and anyone else in the room has a shared understanding of the following:

- What is the outcome the interviewer(s) are looking to evaluate?
- What do the interviewers believe will be the hypothetical impact of the research?
- Are there any specific expectations around how you should operate the exercise?
- What is each person's role in the room, and how are you expected to engage with each?

- How much time should you allocate to each exercise step, and who will track time (you or someone else)?
- If the interviewers are acting as collaborators: are there any questions they would like addressed through your research?

Once you clearly understand expectations around the exercise, you can begin the research conversation or analysis. What that first step looks like will vary—depending on how the company has set up the interview—but in most cases, interviewers will give you a chance to engage with a person or set of collateral related to a specific, often hypothetical problem.

When first engaging with the faux user, setting context around them, their problem or problems, and the environment is vital. To do that effectively, you can rely on time-tested research methods for assessing the interview context:

- Begin by sharing your purpose or goal for the conversation to hear what the customer wants to talk about so you can take the feedback to the team for building or improving solutions.
- Ask what topics the user would like to discuss and what goals they have for the time.
- Explore the user's background and interests related to the business
- Ask the user to walk you through a typical scenario or "day in the life" related to the interview subject.

With a bit of context set between you and the interviewers, you're ready to begin the more formal research process of asking questions, digging deeper into problems and ideas, and synthesizing your findings.

## 12. NAVIGATING USER RESEARCH EXERCISES

Research exercises as part of an interview only differ from real-world research conversations in that they are radically condensed sessions. To successfully navigate a user research exercise in a short time, you will want to ensure you have a shared context on how you should spend the time. Then, listen to the user or evaluate the data effectively, synthesize your insights into themes, and share your research outcomes.

Aligning goals and objectives in the research conversation should be your first task. If possible: repeat them aloud and write them down where you and the interviewer(s) can reference them.

Once you've set and aligned on context, it's time to begin talking with the user. With limited time to conduct the research and synthesize your insights, you want to ensure you focus on the conversation's most essential aspects. Asking the interviewer(s) what the situation is, who matters most, and the research goal will help you focus your conversation on the essential elements. But your goal will be to listen more than you talk.

**Listening to users or evaluating data.**

Research conversations are best when they're lopsided. It would help if you did far more listening at the start than speaking; otherwise, you will struggle to get the insights you need from the conversation.

To listen, you also need something to listen to, and that's where the TEDW framework of question-asking comes into play. By repeatedly asking open-ended questions that begin with phrasing such as:

- Tell me…
- Explain how/why…
- Describe…
- And, Walk me through…

You will get the interviewer/user to open up about their problem or circumstances. Once the conversation starts, it will be your job to continuously ask questions while seeking the user's motivations. You want to understand why there's a problem, what solutions already exist, and why they may be insufficient. But you don't want to ask "why" questions, as doing so will inevitably end up with biased responses from the user and not heart-of-the-matter answers.

As you engage with the user, repeat back what you heard them say to ensure you heard it correctly and that you can hone in on the primary points they are raising.

Finally, rather than taking user preferences as fact, dig deeper. When someone says "I wish..." or "I want..." try not to take their statements as insight. Instead, ask questions to understand why they want the specific thing they share. The underlying motivation for their request is more valuable for you (and the imaginary team you work with within the exercise interview) than blatant user requests.

**Synthesizing insights.**

After (and sometimes during) research conversations, it's essential to synthesize what you've heard—to combine and make sense of ideas. The role of synthesis is to organize and summarize information to identify patterns and relationships. Practical synthesis makes sharing insights with others more accessible than, for example, giving someone a complete list of vague or overly detailed notes.

In the real world, research synthesis can take hours or even days. In a simulated research exercise, you may only have a handful of minutes (if that) to synthesize information. You may also need to synthesize information as you receive it, in real-time, throughout a conversation. One easy way to make sense of information as it comes is to document not an emotion alongside every note. Using a scribbled smiling, sad, or angry face next to a specific word can help you understand the context with which the phrase appeared later in the conversation.

For a user research exercise, you will want to synthesize your notes to create categories or themes of insights. Remember, insights are not merely observations of what you heard in a conversation, but rather: the best insights will explain the motivations a person has and operates within.

When evaluating your notes for insights, pay close attention to anything related to motivation, behavior, challenges for the user, and surprises. If you hear something that surprises you for any reason, that's especially worth highlighting. Otherwise, you will want to capture themes and points from the conversation (or within your data) that deal with goals and objectives. What does the user say they want? How does what they say they want to mirror or contrast with what they do or do not do?

**Sharing findings.**

Lastly, time permitted, you will want to summarize your highlights and significant points or themes back to the mock user and other interviewers. As with any research in the real world: if you can't share your findings in a way that invokes new ideas or gives others a clear path forward, the study may have been suboptimal.

You will want to vocalize your research notes and two or three unique insights for the interview. If you have ideas on what the imaginary team you are on can do with the insights, share those alongside your notes.

At the end of the session, be sure to thank the faux customer for their time, and thank the interviewers for giving you a chance to explore a different perspective and way of thinking.

To recap: You can successfully navigate a user research exercise quickly by ensuring you have a shared context on how you should spend the time. Then, listen to the user or evaluate the data effectively and synthesize your insights into themes. Finally, it would be best if you shared your research outcomes in a way that exemplifies your insights and ideas.

## 13. WHAT ARE EXPLORATORY INTERVIEWS?

In every interview process, you will have a chance to participate in exploratory interviews: open conversations with one or more people about who you are as a designer, how you work with others, your ambitions, and past experiences. Exploratory interviews are often helpful for both companies and job seekers, as such conversations allow both sides to have open discussions around the opportunity and fit.

The purpose of an exploratory conversation is just that: a chance for you and the interviewers to explore the job opportunity through casual conversation. Interviewers will be looking to gather information about you that helps them understand your skills, abilities, and interests, as they overlap with the company's needs and ways of working. Similarly, exploratory interviews are a prime opportunity for you to learn about the company. Coming prepared with questions significant to you will make the conversation go smoothly and demonstrate your seriousness and interest in the job.

Because of their casual nature, exploratory interviews are typically no more than 15 to 30 minutes. Still, they can be as long as an hour if the interviewer is a senior individual, such as a functional head or executive at the company. Interviewers will want to talk to you typically in person, but it's not uncommon for exploratory conversations to occur over the phone or by email. They may be one-on-one or in a group setting. And the interviewer will typically take notes during the interview to record your responses.

While exploratory interviews can take place at any stage of interviewing, they are most common before formally interviewing and late stage. Most common subjects covered in exploratory interviews include discussions about your strengths and areas of opportunity, ambitions for career growth, company culture, collaboration, and more. The conversations will involve cross-functional stakeholders as well as potential collaborators.

During an exploratory interview, the interviewer will evaluate you on any overlapping areas between the job opportunity and your career experience and expectations. Subjects you can anticipate discussing and exploring with interviews include:

- Are you a good fit for the current needs of the company? If not, is there a potential you may be soon?
- Do you have enough relevant experience to navigate the challenges the job will present?
- Are you self-aware; do you know your strengths and how to best leverage them in different situations?
- Will you be happy and fulfilled in the job?
- Is there anything more the company can do to entice you to join?
- Are there any concerns or potential problems that need to be addressed—on either side—before continuing the interview process?
- What types of projects will you thrive in at the company, and what types may require you to have support?

With these subject areas, you can see why some companies prioritize exploratory conversations up-front before a more formal interview process. Others may use late-stage exploratory discussions to " seal the deal" and sell you on the job. In either case: if a company invites you to participate in an exploratory interview, it's essential to be prepared to discuss your qualifications, experiences, and career goals. Additionally, it would help if you came prepared with questions about the company and role.

Exploratory interviews can be less stressful than other parts of the interview process when you look at them for what they are: a chance for the company to get to know you personally and vice-versa.

## 14. HOW TO ENGAGE IN EXPLORATORY INTERVIEWS

An exploratory interview is a meeting between a potential employer and you to discuss the possibility of working together. Interviewers in these conversations usually want a better sense of your qualifications and fit for the position, including how well your ambitions align with what the company can offer.

If you've ever had a job, odds are you've participated in an exploratory interview already in your career. The casual interview format means exploratory conversations are shorter than other interviews, lasting anywhere from 15 minutes to an hour, depending on the role you are applying to and who you speak with in the interview. Companies will often label these interviews with things like: "get to know you," "coffee chat," "values interview," or simply your name/interviewer's name.

Some companies will have multiple exploratory interviews, but it's not uncommon to only have one in addition to a portfolio presentation, design critique, challenge or exercise, and more discussions.

You can tell you're in an exploratory conversation (as opposed to a more rigidly defined interview) by the questions you're asked: interviewers will ask you outright about your qualifications, work experience, and career goals. Interviewers may ask you to describe your ideal job, what you're looking for in your next role, and to explain why you're interested in the specific position you're interviewing for at that time.

Unlike other interviews you will encounter, exploratory discussions do not have a wrong or right answer, nor are there any explicit expectations. Instead, an exploratory conversation seeks to give you and the interviewer a chance to explore the job opportunity in front of you.

So, while these interviews allow employers to learn more about you and your qualifications, they also allow you to discover more about the company and the position. You will want to be prepared to discuss your qualifications and career goals.

Having a handful of stories from our past work or learning experiences will help you through exploratory conversations. Prepare by thinking about some of the most meaningful experiences of your career.

- What are the moments you felt most challenged? What did you do in those situations, and how did you get through them (if you did)? Who helped you? What would you have liked to be different?
- What experiences felt most rewarding to you? What made the experience rewarding?
- When have you found yourself getting along with someone? What made the relationship constructive and helpful?
- What about times you have struggled to work with someone else? What made those collaborations difficult, and how did you respond?

It would help if you also were prepared to ask questions about the company and the position. Some of the question areas you may want to prepare before an exploratory interview include:

- What does the future hold for the role? Is there already a growth ladder in place or an example of someone in a similar position evolving beyond it?
- How does the team handle conflict? Can the interviewer share a recent example of a team conflict and how it got resolved?
- Who makes the most critical decisions on the team (or within the company)? How do those decisions usually get made?
- Where does design sit within the organization? Who decides what success looks like for the function of design, and how are designers evaluated?
- Why is this role open? Why now?
- Who does design collaborate with most in the company, and what is an example of a recent, effective collaboration?

If you ever encounter a situation where you run out of time and cannot ask your questions, you should always ask for more time with the interviewer. Investing in an interview process where you aren't confident of your ability to do well and grow in your career can sabotage you and the company.

In the end, as appropriate, exploratory interviews are best approached by being your authentic self. You don't want to go into the conversation with overly prepared answers, and it shouldn't seem that you are reading from a script at any moment. Be honest and upfront; if you feel comfortable doing so, communicate how you feel throughout the conversation and what you're thinking.

## 15. TALKING ABOUT COLLABORATION IN INTERVIEWS

Collaboration is vital to any job; it makes teams get tasks done efficiently, generate new and innovative ideas, resolve conflicts, and build constructive relationships. Communicating what effective collaboration means to you is a powerful way to get interviewers to see you as a potential teammate rather than merely a job candidate. During exploratory interview conversations, you want the interviewer to be able to imagine themselves working with you, and discussing collaboration is a great way to do just that.

Whether you're working with a team of teammates or clients, effectively communicating and collaborating is essential to your (and the other party's) success. When interviewing, it's crucial to be able to talk about your experiences with collaboration and what makes partnerships challenging or rewarding for you.

Companies may ask you to participate in an interview solely focused on collaboration, but odds are you will need to find ways to speak about collaboration throughout the interview process. Teamwork is vital in any job because it allows teams to share ideas, communicate more effectively, and work toward common goals. When team members collaborate effectively, they can bring their strengths together to be more productive and efficient. As any major league sports team can attest: collaborative teams are winning teams.

When it comes to interviewing, you should be able to talk about your experience with collaboration and what it means to you. Some of the essential areas of collaboration you should come prepared to any interview to speak to include:

- What does collaboration mean to you?
- One or more examples of a collaboration led to success
- One or more instances of a collaboration that was challenging

### What does collaboration mean to you?

When you first begin talking about collaboration, it's essential to define what collaboration means to you. Because collaboration rarely takes the same form between people or teams, it's good to share a brief perspective of what you believe collaboration means before sharing past experiences from your career.

To define collaboration, consider what types of projects you have found yourself working closest with others (both other designers and cross-functional peers). How did you engage with your team members, and what was the outcome of that collaboration? In your own opinion, why do you believe collaboration is important?

You will want to be clear and concise when you speak about collaboration—explain the context of past collaborations, the communication process you used, and how effective or ineffective it was to achieve the team's goals.

The key to talking about collaboration is to share past examples of when a collaboration was a success and when it was more challenging for you. By emphasizing communication methods and how you (and your team members or clients) kept each other informed about what was going on, you can ensure interviewers get the information they need to understand what collaboration means to you.

**Describe a time collaboration led to success.**

When sharing examples of times you've collaborated in the past, it's good to have one or two scenarios ready to go for reference. Think of a time you successfully worked well with someone else. A time you and one or more team members were able to overcome a hurdle or achieve success (even a small victory).

You will want first to share the goal or objective of the collaboration. What were you trying to achieve, and what was the intent of the other person or persons? Once the goals are clear, it can be easier to identify how the collaboration was successful.

What were the key factors, in your opinion, that led to the collaboration being a success? How were you able to communicate effectively with others (and vice-versa)? How did you build and maintain mutual respect between partners? What did you and your team do to establish a shared sense of purpose?

Remember, there is no single best way to collaborate, and no two people or teams will collaborate the same. So your answer to what makes collaboration effective will be reasonably personal. Identifying the key factors that contributed to your past collaboration's success can ensure future collaborations are just as successful.

**Describe a time when collaboration was challenging.**

Not every collaboration comes without its challenges. The longer you are in a career, the more likely you will encounter a situation that inevitably ends in an unsuccessful partnership.

Knowing how much information to share about an unsuccessful or challenging collaboration can be tricky. Still, being honest and open about what went wrong and what you could have done differently is necessary. Unsuccessful partnerships will only reflect poorly on you if you haven't taken the time to think about them retrospectively and identify what you could have tried to make the collaboration more successful.

Before an interview, ensure you have one or two examples of challenging collaborations you have experienced. You will want to also reflect on what you could have done better to make the partnership more successful, regardless of what the other person or people did or did not do.

The most common reasons collaborations can be challenging or unsuccessful include a breakdown in communication, a clash of personalities or working styles, poor project organization, lack of alignment around responsibilities, or disagreement around collaboration objectives.

Once you've identified the cause or causes of the unsuccessful collaboration, you must talk about what you and the team could have done differently. This likely involves taking responsibility for personal mistakes or admitting that the team should have done something differently. It's also important to discuss what you learned from the experience and how you might apply it to future collaborations.

By talking openly and honestly about past collaborations (the good and the bad), it's possible to learn from mistakes and avoid repeating them in the future, leading to more successful projects and better working relationships. That reflection will help interviewers see you not only as a job seeker but as someone who thinks critically about working with others.

# 16. QUESTIONS TO ASK IN INTERVIEWS

There are no "right" or "wrong" questions regarding interviewing. You will likely ask questions based on your career goals, ambitions, and understanding of the job opportunity. Still, it can be helpful and often inspirational to see examples of question areas and specific questions to consider when interviewing.

Ask thoughtful questions during your interview to make a good impression and get your desired job. Thoughtful questions show you're interested in the position and company and that you've thought about what matters most in your career and your ability to collaborate effectively.

Asking questions is also a great way to be engaged in any interview conversation. Sitting passively through every interview sends the message that you're not that interested in the job. On the other hand, if you're asking questions and participating in the conversation, it shows you're engaged and interested in what the interviewer has to say. Some questions can help you make sense of the complexity of the company or job, and others can give you the insight needed to make an informed decision about whether the opportunity is right for you.

Additionally, thoughtful questions can demonstrate your knowledge and expertise. Questions about the company, position, and areas of interest can impress interviewers while getting you answers to questions core to the job.

**Do your research in advance.**

Before your interview, take some time to research the company and role. While it may be tempting to rely on generic questions about the company or the position you're interviewing for, it's important to ask thoughtful questions to help determine if the job is a good fit. A little research can spark thoughtful questions specific to the company and the position.

One way to identify relevant areas of interest is to search online for news about the company or interviews with its executives or design team. A search for "[company name] CEO interview" can help uncover what the business focuses on and even the challenges or opportunities they are encountering. From there, you can use your career goals and abilities to generate questions about how the role you're interviewing for aligns with what the company is trying to achieve.

**Ask about the company culture.**

When it comes to asking questions, you can think of the scale of a job to determine what information you need as it relates to your job decision. Starting at the broadest sense of scale: ask a question about the company itself and the culture it imbues. Some example questions you may want to ask interviewers about the company and its culture include:

- What does the company mission mean to you?
- What challenges has the company recently faced, and how did the team confront them?
- What does the next year look like for the company? What challenges does the company anticipate facing in that time?
- What does cash flow look like for the business? If unsure or unspecific: who is responsible for managing business cash flow, and how do they keep the rest of the company aware of headwinds?
- Who are some of the business's biggest competitors, and what differentiates them?

**Ask about the design function and team.**

The following scale-down in questioning focuses on the design function and the design team itself. Questions to consider asking at this scale are:

- What is the role of design in the company, and how does the company determine design success?
- What trade-offs do you find your team having to make consistently?
- Who is the company's most prominent advocate for design, and how do they show up?

- Where does design contribute the most?
- How are designers on the team evaluated?
- What does the team do if a designer struggles to meet their responsibilities?
- What does it look like for a designer on the team to excel beyond their responsibilities?

**Ask about the day-to-day tasks of the role.**

Finally, focus on the role itself and the day-to-day tasks you might expect to encounter if you were to take the job.

- What unique attributes are you hoping to find in someone for this role?
- What challenges should someone taking this role expect to encounter daily?
- Who will be the closest partners and supporters for someone taking this role?
- How will the daily tasks of this job change over the coming year, if at all?

In the end, thoughtful questions during an interview show that you're genuinely interested in the position and not just going through the motions. With these example questions and frames, you'll be able to ask thoughtful questions that will help you determine if the job is a good fit.

## 17. IMPROVING YOUR COMMUNICATION

Undoubtedly one of the most important aspects of interviewing well is effectively communicating with interviewers. For some, clear and concise communication comes second nature, but others may struggle to convey their ideas and experiences. You can improve your communication by learning to listen to the other people in your conversation, using nonverbal signals, practicing often, and taking time when conveying ideas or experiences to others.

When interviewing, companies are not only looking at your qualifications but also trying to get a sense of who you are as a person. There's no better way to convey your abilities and personality than communicating clearly. Interviewers want to know if you're someone who can speak with others effectively and who will be a positive addition to a team. That's why communication is such an essential aspect of the interview process. If you struggle to communicate well during interviews, you will likely struggle to do the job—this is a broad generalization. Still, there is some universal truth to it, which is why improving communication can make you a more rounded designer and job candidate.

Thankfully, you can do a few things to improve your communication skills before interviewing, and ample resources available to help you.

**What is effective communication?**

Effective communication is challenging for all of us because we each have different ways of perceiving the world. Put bluntly: effective communication is sending and receiving messages to create understanding and achieve objectives. The key to effective communication is to make sure that the message you are sending is the same as the message someone else receives.

We perceive things based on past experiences, beliefs, values, and cultural backgrounds—this means what you think you're saying might be interpreted in different ways by different people.

To ensure you are communicating effectively, you need to take the time necessary to consider and understand the person you are communicating with: what are they seeking, what is their communication style, and what is most important to them at the moment? Once you understand the other person or people you are communicating with, you can tailor your message appropriately to meet their needs.

The best way to ensure effective communication is to listen to the other person's acts and what they say. Is their body language open or closed? Do they repeatedly use certain words or phrases? If you're patient and observant, you can respond to questions and communication with an interviewer in clear and effective ways.

Remember that actively listening does not mean listening to every single word someone else is saying but instead paying attention to the meaning behind the words. If you're unclear about what they're looking for or asking you: ask for clarity.

When you can pair your responses or questions to the specific message of the other person, you will be communicating clearly with them. Clear communication does not always mean being brief or using verbose language. Clear communication will match what the other person is looking for and how they communicate with you.

**Resources to improve communication**

To effectively communicate with someone else is to convey your ideas and experiences concisely, clearly, and easy-to-understand manner. Effective communication requires listening actively to the other person(s), empathy for what they're saying, and using non-verbal communication.

You can improve your communication by first practicing it regularly and in different ways. Practice by sharing your story and experiences in Shape discussions, creating new posts, and responding to others. The more you task yourself with communicating, the more aware you become of your communication habits and effectiveness, and there's no safer way to do that than in a community that seeks to help one another.

Additionally, there are many books, videos, and similar resources you can look to improve your communication:

- Simply Said is a book by Jay Sullivan that presents an all-encompassing guide to improving your communication in life and work.
- HBR's 10 Must Reads on Communication Vol. 2 is a collection of Harvard Business Review articles covering everything from asking better questions to preempting conflict.
- Better Small Talk, by Patrick King, helps unlock your confidence when communicating with others.
- How to Win Friends and Influence People is a timeless book by Dale Carnegie that goes in-depth on applying the basic principles of psychology to your communication.
- Udemy offers a masterclass on Persuasion: how to influence anyone, by Brandon Hakim and Insider School.

If you take just one bit of advice away from this guide for improving communication, make it this: slow down.

Breathe and give yourself the space to understand what's being asked of you or said to you and what your communication should be in return. When speaking aloud, when listening to someone else, take your time.

## 18. THE IMPORTANCE OF PRACTICE INTERVIEWS

Interviews often only give you one chance to make a good impression. Every interview is an opportunity to sell yourself as the best designer for the job. So it's best to prepare. Practicing interviewing can give you confidence, help solidify your stories, and empower you to ask and answer vital questions.

The interview process has become increasingly competitive, with many qualified candidates currently vying for the same positions. The ability to articulate your qualifications and land your desired job relies heavily on confidence, clear communication, and preparedness. If you aren't practicing interviews, you're missing an opportunity to improve each of these things.

You should practice your interview skills if you're looking for a job. Even if you've been interviewing for a long time or have had a lengthy career, your communication and interviewing skills are like a muscle that deteriorates when not used. You can strengthen your interviewing skills by practicing them with a friend, colleague, or partner.

When you practice interviewing, you will build confidence in your ability to communicate and make a good impression. You can prepare by allowing yourself to fine-tune your responses to common interview questions. You will better equip yourself to respond to questions and interview situations (like whiteboard exercises or design critique challenges) and ultimately set yourself up to make a lasting impression with interviewers.

You first want to consider the process and who you practice with to practice your interviewing effectively. Of course, practicing interviews is not as straightforward as looking at yourself in a mirror and talking at yourself (though that is certainly better than not practicing at all). Rehearsing an interview with someone inexperienced may not yield as much insight as practicing with someone who has seen both sides of the interview process—still, some practice is better than none.

You do not need to practice interviewing to memorize a script or establish a routine for how you want to approach every interview conversation. In fact: if your aim in practicing interviewing is to remember anything, you're likely doing yourself a disservice, as interviewers can often tell when something has been rehearsed and memorized.

A strong goal in interviewing should be to clearly convey your skills, abilities, and interests while appearing confident and capable. And the best way to do that is to practice going through interviews.

## 19. HOW TO PRACTICE INTERVIEWING

When it comes to nailing a job interview, preparation goes a long way. The best way to practice interviewing for a job is first to research the company and role, then identify the interview type (behavioral, phone, panel, etc.) and practice with someone who can give you constructive feedback.

To ensure your interviews go smoothly, you will want to practice interviewing with a trusted friend, partner, or peer. But don't simply rehearse a typical interview or ask an inexperienced friend to practice with you. Instead, do your research on the company and role, work to build confidence in your ability to convey what needs to be communicated, and determine how to best respond to specific situations or questions. And, as with most things in life and careers, practice makes perfect.

**To start, do your research.**

Before you practice interviewing, research the common types of interviews you'll be participating in and who will likely be in the conversation. You can plan if you know who you'll be chatting with and what subjects they'll cover. Some of the most common interview types you can prepare for generically include:

- Exploratory conversations
- Problem-solving exercises
- Portfolio presentations
- Design critiques
- Past work reviews

If you already know who you'll be talking to, you can research the specific individuals and their roles. Look at the interviewer's LinkedIn profile to see where they've worked in the past and their current title—this will give you a better sense of what they may be responsive to in an interview.

Even if you don't know who you'll be speaking to, you can prepare more generally by understanding the most common roles involved in the interview process and what they tend to care most about through interview conversations.

**Plan for common interview questions.**

After you've done a small amount of research, it's time to start preparing for the actual interviews you'll go through. One of the best ways to do this is by finding answers to common interview questions. Of course, you won't be able to predict every question interviewers will ask, but you can prepare for the most common ones. Some examples of common interview questions include:

- Can you tell me a little bit about yourself?
- What are your strengths? What are your weaknesses?
- Why are you interested in this position?
- What makes you qualified for this job?
- What are your long-term career goals?
- What is it about this company that appeals to you?
- What are your thoughts on design practices and processes?
- What would you do if someone gave you critical feedback?
- Can you share a time you failed a project?

As with any interview: you do not want to memorize answers to these questions. Instead, use the act of practice to build confidence in having an appropriate response. When it comes time to answer one of these or similar questions, you do not want to sound rehearsed but instead confident and ready to provide insight into your experience and abilities.

**Practice with someone experienced in interviewing.**

Once you have a solid understanding of the company and the role you're interviewing for and have prepared answers to common interview questions, it's time to start practicing. If you can, find someone who can role-play as the interviewer and run through a mock interview with you; this will help you get comfortable with the format and flow of an interview and give you a chance to practice your answers aloud.

Before diving into a mock interview, you will want to prepare in three ways:

1. Know what you want to learn or improve from your practice. Are you seeking to communicate more clearly? Do you want to provide examples more readily to interview questions? Or something else?
2. Ensure the person you're practicing with has experience interviewing. Interviews are unique types of conversations in that they aim to get a signal on specific criteria without "giving away the plot." Practiced and trained interviewers know how to ask questions and interpret responses according to specific evaluation criteria, whereas inexperienced people may view the interview as merely another conversation.
3. Find a way to record the conversation or take notes. It isn't easy to improve on something you aren't actively reflecting on, so if possible: use your phone or computer to record the conversation and listen to it afterward.

If you don't have anyone to practice with, that's okay! You can still do a mock interview on your own. Just pretend you're being interviewed by someone and go through the motions. The more you practice, the more confident you'll feel going into your actual interview, and the more likely you will effectively navigate conversations that can make or break a job offer.

# FIVE
# DECISION MAKING

## 1. SETTING COMPENSATION EXPECTATIONS

Many job seekers don't feel comfortable discussing compensation during the interview process, but not doing so could cost you. When you don't set expectations around compensation for a role, or when the company you're interviewing with doesn't have clear expectations, it can create a disconnect and lost opportunity on both sides.

When it comes to compensation, the first thing to do is set expectations for yourself before discussing any numbers with a company. You can't set reasonable compensation expectations before setting expectations for yourself. However, it's also essential to understand an interested company's compensation bands in order to calibrate your own.

**Start with research.**

In many places, compensation is taboo: talking about payment is shunned by both companies and designers for many reasons. Fear of offending someone, identifying inequitable or unfair compensation, coming across as overly financially motivated, and simply being uncomfortable discussing money keeps people from the open dialog about compensation.

Thankfully, compensation is becoming a more accepted point of conversation. As a result, we can research and establish expectations around what companies pay.

**Note:** As I was writing this guide, New York and other cities across the United States have begun passing laws wherein compensation must be included in all job posts. You can reference these statistics in your search and when making decisions!

When evaluating expectations for your compensation, the first thing should be to look at your financial needs and existing compensation (if you have any income). Every other attribute of compensation research will not matter if you can't pay your bills and feed yourself or those you care for, so start by defining, on paper, your financial needs.

Once you have an initial idea of your needs, you can look to external resources to determine what reasonable compensation seems like for the types and levels of jobs you seek. These resources allow anyone in the world to self-report their compensation and therefore provide others with the information needed to evaluate relative compensation expectations:

- Levels.fyi provides global compensation numbers across a myriad of companies, big and small.
- Glassdoor.com is a historically `central place for checking compensation across various companies, though leans more toward technology companies.
- LinkedIn.com job posts occasionally include compensation ranges aggregated across LinkedIn for similar jobs.
- Payscale.com does not rely solely on self-reported data and is often more reliable than crowdsourced resources for compensation data.

Because individuals self-reporting compensation are the source of information for many of these resources, they are not always reliable. You should not use these resources as references when negotiating salary. Instead, use open source compensation data to balance your personal needs and additional research methods, including what the company has set for their compensation range.

**Ask the company for their compensation bands.**

There is no more reliable source for compensation expectations than the company you are interviewing with. While most companies will provide compensation bands to designers, they will not do so readily and may require coaxing.

Companies often have a leg-up on designers in this regard, because they have inside information on compensation and should have an idea of total compensation for the role. Companies often use industry research firms that specialize in auditing, understanding, and sharing compensation values across companies and industries—such as Radford. The company will also likely have internal pay bands that try to create equitable pay across functions and teams, with pre-approved budget allocated for roles.

When it comes to discussing compensation, you should feel empowered to prod the company for what their expectation is around the role. You can politely and carefully ask for compensation or respond to an interviewer asking you about salary by saying:

"I have considered my compensation expectations, but I would like to know what you have set for compensation bands before I share my thoughts. From my information, I am excited about the opportunity; but I want to ensure my compensation expectations align with your internal numbers."

In some cases, you may need to repeatedly ask the interviewer to share their ideas and compensation expectations before you get an answer. Still, persist until you get a number, then use that number to inform what happens next.

**Be honest about where you're at with expectations.**

With a bit of research and clear expectations, you can engage in compensation conversations with more honesty and accuracy to get what you need and want. Evaluate your research with the company's shared compensation bands by asking yourself questions such as:

- Is the company's band more or less than you need?
- How flexible are you capable of being regarding compensation and, if needed, can you advocate for your expectations?
- Is the compensation considerably more or less than what you've found through other resources?
- Would a signing bonus or stock equity dramatically change the compensation amount?

Depending on the answers to those questions, you can share your highest expectations with the company and begin the compensation negotiation process.

## 2. NAVIGATING JOB REQUIREMENTS

Understanding job requirements is essential before engaging with interviewers or accepting a job offer. While it may sound obvious, many designers forgo investing time to understand what a company will expect of them. When you know the job requirements fully, you can have confidence the job is a good fit for your skills and experience and that you're able to meet the expectations of the job.

Experienced designers often feel they have a good grasp of job responsibilities regarding interviewing. Yet, no two companies operate the same, and no two roles will be identical.

One primary point of interviewing is demonstrating your skills and ability to do a job. Another is determining whether or not what a company expects of the position aligns with what you offer. Spending a bit of time researching, getting clarity, and reflecting on the responsibilities of a job you are interested in can save you (and the company) a lot of pain in the future.

To navigate job requirements before and during interviews, look beyond the job description and into the company itself, be honest with yourself and interviewers about your abilities to meet needs, and ask questions during interviews to get clarity on any unclear job requirements. Interviewers often understand that job posts and conditions are not always explicitly clear. Asking for clarity about anything you read or hear about a job only strengthens your ability to prepare for interviews and eventual hire.

Of course, navigating job requirements is complicated when you aren't first aware of your strengths, weaknesses, and (critically) career goals. Before applying to jobs, evaluating jobs, and interviewing, it's important to re-visit your career goals. Is there anything about your career trajectory that you need to re-evaluate? Are there jobs that are more aligned with your career goal than others?

It can be helpful to take your career goals and assess them against job posts and descriptions outright, looking for things like similar phrasing for job responsibilities and requirements. Consider exploring the following questions for yourself:

- Does the job post include identical language (or synonyms) to your skills and what you're looking for?
- Do interviewers use consistent language that aligns with the job post?
- Is there anything in the job post that defines a responsibility you need clarity on?
- Do you know how the company culture and values support the expected job responsibilities?
- Have you talked with someone with similar responsibilities as what's listed to get a sense of real-world interpretation?

Lastly, it's critical to understand what listed job requirements mean and do not mean.

One of the most significant areas of self-rejection from a job post is years of experience and expected education. Job seekers often misinterpret these areas, and research has shown that women tend not to apply to jobs unless they meet 100% of the listed requirements, whereas men will apply to any job they feel they meet at least 60% of the listed requirements.

While there is no single best approach for applying to a job, it is always worth applying to a job you feel meets at least 60% of the requirements. And if you don't have the number of years of experience or education requirements? Apply anyway.

Often, years of experience are shorthand a company will use when posting a job. They are usually not looking for someone with exactly or more than the years of experience listed on a job post. Instead, they use "years of experience" to convey they are eager to get someone with working knowledge that someone with that many years of experience may have picked up.

In other words: years of experience is shorthand for, "We want someone who will have experience dealing with the types of things a designer at this level will have." Years of experience is hardly ever a rigid, explicit requirement for a job.

By taking the time to understand the job requirements, you ensure you don't end up in a job that's not a good fit for your ambitions and skills.

## 3. UNDERSTANDING CAREER GROWTH FROM INTERVIEWS

Every worthwhile job offers you a chance to do great work and be compensated for it, but excellent jobs will also allow you to grow in your career. You can use interviews to understand career growth opportunities for a specific company or role and your assessment to determine if the job is right for you.

Particularly when evaluating one job against another, knowing which opportunity will give you the ability to grow in your career and achieve your career goals can help you decide to pursue or decline an interview or job offer. Career growth doesn't always have to equate to a vivid pathway toward becoming an executive or something similar. Instead, it's best to think of career growth as an increase in your ability to do your job over time and, critically, achieve your career goals.

Career growth is crucial as it can lead to increased job satisfaction, higher compensation, and a sense of stability or progress in your work. Companies typically invest in career growth opportunities for designers, leading to increased loyalty and productivity.

You can define career growth on the job through outcomes such as salary, job satisfaction, increased responsibility or promotions, and recognition. But when you're interviewing for a job, it can be hard to get a signal on career growth. Though you can gain an understanding of possible career growth from interviews by researching the company and its business model, being clear about your career goals and ambitions, and asking questions about situations or examples of what career growth looks like at the company.

**Researching and understanding company growth.**

Career growth ultimately stems from company growth; when a company is doing well and growing, it creates more opportunities for designers to grow.

When it comes to interviewing, a little research can go a long way, and that mantra also applies to understanding career growth opportunities. Please research the company and its business model before and during interviews. Look into articles and public resources that talk about the company's financial trajectory, its competition, and how it might be aiming to grow in the coming years.

Researching a company on resource websites like Glassdoor.com and Crunchbase.com, or searching online for articles mentioning things such as "[Company name] funding" or "[Company name] CEO interview" can tell you a lot about the company's current trajectory and possible future.

Smaller companies can offer great career growth as long as the company trajectory is optimistic and can support employees over the coming years. Career growth in larger companies can be difficult— depending on your goals—but can be determined by questioning what the company does for those who excel in their roles, and what those types of individuals look like within the company.

**Revisit your career goals.**

If you're interviewing and haven't yet set your career goals, it can be challenging to know which jobs are best suited for you and vice-versa. Having a clear career goal can better align what you're looking for in a position with what opportunities are out there.

During an interview, clearly communicate your career goals and what you want to achieve in the job. Through interviews, employers often help align your expectations and ambitions with what they offer or clarify when there isn't a good fit. And while the feeling of risking being declined a job offer due to a mismatch between your goals and the job can seem frightening, it's a simple way to avoid a potentially hazardous and painful career experience later down the road.

When communicating your career goals in interviews, make it clear that you are open to opportunities and willing to prioritize one thing over another. However, your ambitions are there to help align you with options.

**Ask for examples of career growth.**

Finally, one of the best ways to understand career growth while interviewing is to ask for examples of times the company helped someone grow. Companies will ask you for examples of times you used skills and abilities to do a job, and you can explore their job offers the same way. Consider some of the following questions for getting a signal on career growth opportunities when interviewing:

- Can you share a recent time someone in the company grew through a promotion or increased responsibilities? How did they get to that point, and what did that growth opportunity look like before?
- What does the company offer regarding formal training and career development for designers?
- What do promotions look like at the company, and how are promotion cases determined? Who determines if a promotion is warranted or not?
- What is the company policy on role changes? How does the company react if a designer wants to transition to a management position (or vice-versa)?
- How has the company grown over the past [N] years? How will the organization grow in the next [N] years?
- What will someone in this role be doing a year from now?
- What does the designer career path look like at the company today? Is there a leveling rubric or framework you can share with me?

Career growth is essential for employees and companies alike. By helping designers grow in their careers, companies create environments that foster innovative thinking, high job satisfaction, and more. Knowing what support for your career growth might look like at a company you're interviewing with can give you additional confidence when deciding to pursue or decline a job.

## 4. WHAT HAPPENS AFTER INTERVIEWING

The interview process is only one step of many in the journey to getting a job. After your final interview, a few things must happen to finalize the process. The interview group will discuss observations and concerns. The hiring manager will evaluate all feedback and decide to either extend an offer, not make an offer or conduct more interviews with you.

Once you've finished your final interview with a company, you often are left with little more than to wait. It can be difficult and frustrating to invest so much time in talking with a company about a job, only to be left wondering how long the decision process will take. From the company's perspective, understanding what happens after interviewing can help you understand why it can often take some time for a decision to be made (or, other times, why a company might make a decision almost instantly).

Companies today know that shorter interview cycles—and decisions—lead to better outcomes for everyone involved. Yet, because the final stages of interviewing and decision-making require multiple people, getting everyone aligned on an outcome can take some time. This can mean a company will take anywhere from one to several days to get back to you on whether or not they would like to extend you a job offer.

Here's what is happening behind the scenes:

**The interviewing group debriefs.**

Shortly after your final interview (typically the same day or no more than one business day later), everyone involved in your final interview conversations will submit feedback through an Applicant Tracking System. In most cases, the team will have already defined evaluation criteria, and interviewers merely need to write an overview of the conversation they had with you and identify anything that stood out as being good or bad from it.

To ensure every bit of feedback is considered in context, the group will meet together (in real life or over video) to rapidly discuss and review your qualifications and performance across the interview process. Interview debriefs can be as short as 15 minutes (if there's an apparent positive or negative reflection of you) or as long as an hour (if there are conflicting or vague assessments).

The hiring manager on the job has the final say on whether a job offer makes sense or not, so they will want to have as much detail as possible from everyone who interviewed you. After reminding the interviewing group what the company is looking for in a candidate, and why the role is essential, they will ask the group questions about the conversation.

After the hiring manager has collected feedback, they will work with the recruiter to either make an immediate decision or have a separate, brief conversation to discuss. Additional discussions will cover the positives and negatives of extending an offer, anything related to compensation or timelines, and how the decision will be communicated.

**The hiring manager evaluates all feedback with the recruiter.**

Throughout the interview debrief and recruiter-hiring manager discussion, the hiring manager and recruiter will be paying close attention to the following questions:

- Do you have the skills to ramp up and progress on the job as quickly as possible?
- Will you need internal help—at the expense of the company— to be able to perform the job duties? Is that something the team can provide or not?
- Does how you presented yourself, your values, goals, and your skills align with how the company likes designers to operate?
- Were any negative signals related to your skills, communication, etc., that may create cultural problems on the team?
- Are you as enthusiastic about the opportunity as the team is?
- Are others in the interview group possibly excited to work with you, or would anyone feel sad if you didn't join the team?

Not every evaluation looks at these criteria, but most do. And while not every hiring manager will lean on their recruiter to help them make a decision, in healthy teams, the hiring manager and recruiter align on a decision before they make a decision. (Just one reason of many to treat recruiters with the utmost respect throughout interviewing.)

In some cases, there may not be enough information to make a decision. The hiring manager may decide not to extend an offer or to set up additional interviews to gather other signals.

**The hiring manager reviews the criteria for a decision.**

If the hiring manager and team feel they did not get enough information from you during the interview process to make a clear decision, they may decide not to go forward with extending an offer. This is occasionally the result of interest in the role, intense competition, or poor processes. However, in most cases, the company may ask you to return for another interview or round of exploratory discussions.

Additionally, as part of the interviewing group debrief, the team may debate internally whether a negative signal (such as poor performance during a design challenge) resulted from nervousness, lack of ability, or something else.

Everyone involved in the process wants to ensure a timely decision because any time spent debating or clarifying has considerable financial costs for the company. However, strong hiring managers also know that making a poor decision could result in a bad experience for the new hire and a poor external reputation when it comes to hiring in the future.

So hiring teams must balance the need to make an informed decision with the need to make a prompt one. Add in the complexity of scheduling multiple people to provide feedback and discuss notes from past interviews, and you can see why some decision-making processes can take time. A rapid decision can mean something in the interview process was glaringly poor, or it could mean the company isn't willing to invest more in determining whether you could do the job well. The decision is about how much information you could effectively provide the company for their needs. Rejection does not always mean you interviewed poorly or are incapable of doing the job you interviewed for, only that the information created the perception of a mismatch between the company and you.

**A recruiter communicates the decision to you.**

If the interview decision is not to extend a job offer, typically, the recruiter (though on occasion the hiring manager) will send you an email or request a call with you.

As eager as you might be to get feedback when rejected from a job, the company is likely very busy with additional interviews. Companies refrain from giving rejected candidates feedback because they don't want to expose themselves to a possible lawsuit (particularly in the United States) or spend time debating someone on their skills. Instead of asking for feedback (if not readily given), use resources like Shape to reflect on and evaluate your interviews.

If the decision is favorable, the recruiter will likely ask you to do a phone call with them (and occasionally the hiring manager). During the call, the recruiter will extend an offer to you, but that doesn't necessarily mean you got the job. A vocal offer means you have the opportunity to take the chance.

**Negotiation begins.**

After a recruiter shares a vocal job offer with you, negotiating begins. The recruiter will want to finalize a potential start date and compensation and align on any outstanding items such as title, responsibilities, work location, etc. You can negotiate almost everything with the company and should seriously consider doing so to align your needs with them.

Suppose you've made it this far. Congratulations! The odds are you were one of hundreds or thousands of people to work your way through an interview process and get the offer. You should feel proud of your ability to convey your skills and abilities effectively, even before negotiations begin.

## 5. VOICING CONCERNS LATE IN THE PROCESS

It can be frightening to voice any concerns during an interview, particularly if you're in the late stages of the process. However, it's essential to remember that having questions or concerns about a job is expected, and thoughtful questions can lead to positive interactions with interviewers. Voicing your concerns and questions respectfully and professionally can give you the information you need to decide on what to do next about a job opportunity.

If you've made it to late-stage interviews at a company, you haven't crossed the finish line into more relaxing territory with interviewers. Still, it would be best if you weren't afraid to ask hard questions and voice any concerns.

Perhaps you feel that one of the interviewers neglected your answers or wasn't giving you their full attention. Or maybe you are concerned that the company hasn't allowed you to express what matters most to you in a career. Your concerns may entail worries over compensation, a sense of poor team collaboration or ill-defined processes, or opportunities for career growth.

Whatever your concerns, it's essential to raise them with the recruiter, hiring manager, or appropriate interviewer as soon as possible. To present your problems effectively, consider the following.

**Make sure your concerns are clear.**

If something is concerning to you, figure out the concern and why it's important to you before discussing it with an interviewer or recruiter. If you're unsure what's at the heart of your concern, take a moment to write down your thoughts before articulating them in conversation. You can also confide in a close friend or peer to make sense of a complex or uncertain situation.

**Bring up any concerns early in the interview process.**

Where possible, bring up any concerns and uncertainties you have as soon as possible. The sooner you raise concerns, the sooner you can get a sense of whether the job is a good fit for you—and vice-versa.

Remember that a recruiter's job is to help evaluate and bring talented designers into the company, which means they want to ensure you have a positive experience interviewing. When in doubt, ask the recruiter if you could set up a time to discuss any concerns.

**Be respectful and professional when voicing concerns.**

When it's time to raise your concerns or ask the questions you've had in the back of your mind, remember to do so respectfully and professionally; you want to avoid being hostile or aggressive, instead focusing on expressing your concerns as calmly and clearly as possible. Instead of saying something akin to, *"I'm worried about the team dynamics,"* try something like, *"I'm excited to work with the team, but I want to make sure we can mesh well together."* This way, you show that you're still interested in the job and able to communicate your concerns.

**Ask for clarification if needed.**

If you're unsure about something during an interview, do not be afraid to ask for clarification. You may worry that asking for clarity can come across as being naive or inexperienced. Still, when you ask for clarification about something, it is often interpreted as taking the interview process seriously. Thoughtful questions can come across as engaging conversation and allow you to learn more about the position to determine if it's right for you. Teams want someone interested in the company, role, and process, and asking for clarity when needed exemplifies those points.

When interviewing for a job, being candid and honest about your thoughts and feelings is important. However, it would help if you were tactful and respectful of the company and interviewers.

## 6. NEGOTIATING JOB OFFERS

Landing a job offer can feel like a victory in any job search (and rightly so), but it's important to remember that companies don't set everything on an offer in stone until both parties agree and sign to it. Most employers expect some negotiation regarding compensation, start date, and perks.

It's no secret that job seekers who don't negotiate their salary are leaving money on the table. A study by Salary.com found that a whopping 75% of employees who didn't negotiate their salary regretted it later.

Pushing back on an offer will not always lead to the company rescinding it; that rarely happens due to negotiations. If a company has gone through the interview process with you and invested in getting you an offer, you would have to ask for something unrealistic to have them change their mind.

Companies that provide job offers have already decided they want you on their team! What remains is to get things like start date, compensation, and perks aligned with what you need or want and what the company can offer. Negotiation is a natural part of the job process. Even if the offer the company has given you is what you wanted (or better), it can only benefit you to try and negotiate further.

There are many reasons why it's almost always beneficial to negotiate about a job. For one, it shows you're confident in your skills and experience. Additionally, negotiating an offer allows you to ask for what you deserve or need in your career. If you're unsure how to negotiate a job offer with your potential employer, follow these steps.

**Express gratitude, but don't say yes right away.**

Don't feel pressured to accept the offer immediately—after all, the employer expects you to negotiate. It's ok to say, *"I am excited about this offer and confident in taking it. However, I want to make sure I am considering everything so will need a day to get back to you, if that's alright?"*

Recruiters will almost always be willing to grant you at least a day to process an offer, if not more time, as long as you're communicating clearly with them about your thinking and why you want the additional time. Do not string a company along in hopes of getting a better offer from a different company or out of hopes you can make them worry about your decision. Honesty is the best policy, and if a company gets a sense you are not being truthful about how you feel toward the business or offer, they may implore you to decide immediately or eventually rescind the offer.

**Do your research.**

Before and during interviews, you should already have completed some research on what to expect from an offer. Your research should include expectations around title and responsibilities as well as compensation and benefits.

Once a company makes you an offer—either formally on paper or informally, vocally—you will want to revisit your research on what a realistic salary looks like for the position. Several websites can help you evaluate salary and compensation expectations, such as Glassdoor.com, Salary.com, and Levels.fyi. Once you have a good idea of the going rate and how it compares to your offer, think about how much you're willing to accept.

It's important to note that public repositories of compensation are often self-reported and not always reliable. Please do not rely on these resources as fact. Instead, use public resources to get a general understanding of compensation for a role, match it with your personal needs, and calibrate based on what a company offers you.

An employer will rarely offer their best possible deal right off the bat. Don't be afraid to counteroffer if you receive an offer lower than you hoped. It's important to remember that there's room for negotiation, and you shouldn't accept an offer that doesn't meet your needs.

**Be prepared to compromise.**

While knowing your worth is essential, you must also be prepared to compromise. For example, if the company is willing to provide a specific annual bonus as part of the offer, but you were hoping for a premium that's ~10% higher, be prepared to accept the amount they initially offered and try to negotiate for other benefits. Compromise is, after all, a cornerstone of any good relationship, at work or otherwise.

Remember that compensation is not just base pay. You can also negotiate for a signing bonus (a percent of the proposed salary, to be given upon signing the offer, with some minor stipulations), annual bonuses or stock grants, more vacation days, flexible working hours, and more. Take each of these things into consideration as you approach negotiations.

**Be polite and professional.**

Even if you believe the company's offer is considerably lower than what you have researched, remember that external research is rarely entirely accurate. The company will know what it can realistically offer. Of course, if you feel like they are lowballing you, don't be afraid to walk away from the offer. A tough decision that can sometimes be necessary to get what you need or deserve.

Remember, as you negotiate a job offer, you are not trying to offend the employer; you're simply trying to get the best possible situation. If the company counters your counter, don't hesitate to negotiate further. The goal is to reach an agreement both parties are happy with, and both sides want the same outcome.

You should be confident in your negotiations and be ready to provide evidence of what you ask for (such as research, references, or examples of your past accomplishments and experiences).

I personally recommend asking for at least 5% above the initial compensation for any job offer when in doubt. While you may not get the amount you ask for, you are guaranteed not to get it if you don't ask.

## 7. EVALUATING JOB OFFERS

When you've been looking for a job and interviewing for a while, it can be tempting to jump at the first offer you receive. However, it's essential to take some time to evaluate a job offer carefully before deciding. If you don't assess the offer, you may end up in a position you weren't prepared for or otherwise expecting.

You might think it's obvious to step back and reflect on a job offer and the benefits and challenges it might bring, yet most of us generally don't do it. The interviewing process can be long and wear you down —not to mention the overall process of searching for a job. So, when a company makes you an offer, you might feel like it's an opportunity to stop your search, cancel any remaining interviews with other companies, and accept it.

But what happens if you take a job only to discover the team culture isn't what the company advertised during interviews? Or what if you start that new job and realize the responsibilities are well more (or less) than you're qualified for at the time?

According to a 2011 Careerbuilder study, 80% of company turnover is partially due to a mismatch. A mismatch between what the company and the new hire expected of one another. Companies invest considerable time and resources in ensuring they're hiring the best designer for a job, and you should put in the same effort to evaluate the job offer.

What should you look at in a job offer to ensure it's right for you?

**Salary and benefits for today and in the future.**

One of the most important factors to consider when evaluating a job offer is the salary and benefits package—the "total compensation." Ensure you understand the position's salary range and any included benefits or stock grants. Look beyond the flat salary or even the aggregate amount of total compensation.

Then, look beyond the immediate compensation into the years ahead. If you aren't clear on what salary increases look like at the company, ask the recruiter or hiring manager. Does the company conduct annual performance reviews that determine salary increases? Is there any inflation budget for yearly increases? How are promotions and other benefits evaluated and determined?

**Company culture and immediate team.**

Another essential factor to consider when evaluating a job offer is the company culture. Please research the company and try to find out its values and priorities, in addition to speaking to members of your potential immediate team.

If the recruiter hasn't given you a chance to speak with team members while interviewing, you can ask to set up simple calls with one or more of them. You should also seek casual, get-to-know-you calls with cross-functional team members, your future direct manager, and anyone else the company sees as evangelists for their culture.

When talking to each person, see if they are a good match for your values and working style. What are they most excited about when it comes to having a new team member? What would they hope someone like you can help with sooner than later? How will they support you, your career ambitions, and your learning needs?

**Work responsibilities and expectations.**

Of course, you will also want to consider the actual work you will be doing in the role. Throughout the interview process, you should have gotten examples of the job's responsibilities and expectations for evaluating success.

If you have any remaining questions or are unsure about what responsibilities may look like as you ramp up on the job, talk with the recruiter and hiring manager about getting clarity.

What does a successful first month look like for the job? What will the first three months be like on the job? How does the company evaluate employee performance, and are there any career ladders or leveling frameworks/rubrics they can share with you in advance?

## 8. WHAT TO DO WHEN YOU HAVE MULTIPLE JOB OFFERS

How do you select from multiple job offers when trying to figure out which is best for you? You can make a more informed and aligned decision by looking at your career goals and comparing each offer's company culture, work/life balance, location, development opportunities, projects, team beliefs, and compensation and benefits package.

For many designers, getting a job offer can be a career-changing experience. But what happens if you get more than one offer? The added excitement and pressure around multiple job offers can make it challenging to evaluate and decide which one is best for you.

Selecting from multiple job offers is ultimately a personal choice, which makes the decision process all the more difficult. Every job offer will offer something different, and your values, principles, skills, and ambitions can be most helpful in picking between more than one offer. Asking a friend or mentor for help navigating your options can be beneficial, but only in so much as you are already aware of what matters most to you personally and professionally.

**Reflect on your career goal.**

Before interviewing, investing time in figuring out your career goals is crucial. When you have clear career goals to work toward, you are much more capable of identifying and pursuing opportunities that align with you. If you aren't clear on what you're trying to do with any job direction, you're much more likely to take any job that comes your way—which isn't always a good thing, nor is it always bad.

When you get multiple job offers, often it's coming back to the career goal that will help you decide which direction is best. Remember that a job can provide security and financial sustenance and act as a stepping stone to more or better opportunities for yourself. Compensation, perks, and team culture are all critical, but they pale compared to a chance that will help you get where you want to go in your career. So start any evaluation of multiple job offers by thinking about and, if needed, asking the recruiter and hiring manager questions about your career goal.

### Chart each job's pros and cons.

When you know what's important to you in a job and how multiple offers stack up against each, making a decision becomes much more manageable.

A tried-and-true practice for evaluating multiple job opportunities is to create a written list or table comparing aspects of each job. These lists commonly include compensation, location, company culture, development opportunities, growth opportunities, team leadership, work/life balance, and more.

The goal of creating a list isn't to document each offer but also to capture your feelings or intuition about each pro or con. For example: rather than merely writing "$120,000 base salary" for one offer, you would write the salary number *and* an emoji or number (1 through 3) to document how that number feels to you. When you look at the cumulative numbers for each offer, you'll have a better sense of which one offers you the most—on your terms.

Tools like Teal can help you not only track and compare multiple offers but also help you track every job you apply to and the details of each.

### Address your core questions.

If you're still struggling to evaluate multiple job offers after comparing their pros and cons and reflecting on your career goal, here are several questions you can address to help.

1. What are the company cultures like? Do you prefer a more traditional corporate environment or a start-up culture?
2. What is the work/life balance like at each company?
3. What is the office location like (if applicable)? And what would a commute entail (if applicable)?
4. What are the development opportunities like? Does one job offer more training and development opportunities than another?

5. What are the projects you would be working on?
6. What are the team's beliefs around success? And how does the team manager support and grow individual designers?

## 9. HOW HIRING DECISIONS GET MADE

Despite how it may seem, hiring decisions are never made in a single moment. Instead, hiring decisions evolve throughout interviews and many debriefs with interviewers. If you want to calm your nerves after interviewing or set yourself up for what might come next, here's a look at how many hire / no-hire decisions get made.

When making hiring decisions, companies usually have a process that involves multiple steps and checkpoints. Having multiple checkpoints and interview stages ensures that the decision makers consider all of the necessary factors before making a final choice.

For each step of the recruiting process, the interviewers and hiring team (often a recruiter and a hiring manager, but sometimes more than that) will work together to evaluate feedback and criteria. If there are positive indications that someone can meet the needs of the business (and vice-versa!), the hiring team will approve the candidate to move to the next stage of the process, of course.

It's at the end of the recruiting process when you've done a batch day of interviews and presented your work to a panel of interviewers where the most major decision gets made: are all of the previous positive signals enough to warrant giving the candidate an offer?

Sometimes, the decision may be relatively easy for the hiring manager and recruiter to make. But often, several strong and capable candidates will be vying for the same position. In these instances, companies must take their time and consider all the factors before making a final decision.

Relying on a single interview, presentation, portfolio of work, or experience, is often not enough to make an informed decision. So companies will depend on multiple interviews, reviewing a broad swath of work and experiences, professional references, and even (in some cases) social media feeds before deciding to hire someone or not for a job.

Companies will also often be aware of personal biases when making hiring decisions. We all have our personal preferences and prejudices.

Still, companies must set these aside when evaluating candidates for a job to ensure the best possible candidate rather than someone people merely "like" or are personally connected with. For example, if the company prefers people like themselves in terms of age, race, gender, or educational background, they may unwittingly exclude qualified candidates who differ. It is crucial to consciously combat these biases by considering all qualified candidates equally regardless of their characteristics. Companies will use a myriad of tools and processes to manage.

The types of information a hiring manager and their recruiter may optimize their decision by includes:

- Is this person experienced enough to deal with the situations they will likely encounter on the job?
- Does this person have the skills needed to do the job well and, if possible, above average?
- Will this person require much time to "ramp up" on our business and processes? Or do we think they may "hit the ground running" after some initial onboarding?
- Were there any concerns from interviewers about this person's demeanor or decorum? Was this person able to present themselves professionally, authentically, and with enthusiasm about our company?
- Were there any concerns from interviewers about how this person would affect our team culture? Does it seem like the person has something to add to our culture or something that may create an unfavorable environment for others (such as ego or nepotism)?
- Is this person proactive and energized by their work, or are they the type of person who will need a lot of instruction?
- Can we afford to pay and support this person for the amount of work and impact they will have on our company?
- Is there another candidate who meets more of these requirements than this one?

The purpose of interviewing is to get answers to these questions as quickly and effectively as possible. The more information the company has about you, the easier it can decide whether to hire you.

If you align well with these questions, you will likely get a hire decision. If not, companies will either decide to try and get more information or, in most cases, cut their losses and continue interviewing other candidates.

If you check each of these questions but so do one or more other designers, the decision may come down to whoever can negotiate the best or has the most relevant experience or skills. Companies will want to hire someone who best aligns with what they can offer and the type of company they want to build, and the closer you are to that, the better your odds of getting a job offer.

Of course, you should work to build your own set of internal questions to gauge your hire decision for companies too.

# 10. HOW TO DEAL WITH JOB REJECTION

When you get rejected from a job, it can hurt and often be a confusing state to be in if the interviewers didn't give you much of a reason for the rejection. It's easy to feel defeated after even one rejection, let alone multiple, and you might question your skills and ambitions as a designer. Thankfully, rejection rarely is about us as individuals.

When a company sends you a rejection notice (or stops communicating with you), remember that the rejection is not about you, what you're capable of, or an indicator of you being any less than somebody else.

Rejection is a mismatch between you and a specific job. That's it.

It's no secret that the job market is hugely competitive. With so many talented and qualified designers vying for the same position, it's no wonder employers are getting more selective in their hiring process. So, if a company rejects you at any stage of the process, don't take it personally. Instead, try to use rejection as an opportunity to learn and grow.

Even if the company rejected you without telling you why, there are many things you can do on your own to evaluate the situation, identify what you might do to improve and increase your chances of getting hired in the future.

**Trust your gut.**

Was there something you felt you could have done better in the interview process? Did you invest enough research and effort into this particular job? Maybe you struggled most in selling yourself during an interview. If you want to land a job, you need to be able to convince the employer that you're the best person for the role. This means being able to articulate your strengths and accomplishments clearly and confidently. It also means being prepared to answer any tough questions that come your way.

We're usually right when we sense something could have gone better while interviewing.

Knowing something went wrong is different from learning how to improve. But if you have an intuition that you could have done something better or differently, take that as a starting point to investigate further. Share the situation and your gut feeling with a mentor or peer or in a Shape discussion to get other perspectives and help.

**Consider the company culture.**

One of the most common reasons for rejection is simply because the company wasn't a good fit. Maybe the culture didn't align with your values, or the position wasn't what you expected. Perhaps the company had shifting priorities that changed what they needed from the job. Whatever the reason, it's important to remember that not every company matches you.

The most glaring difference will be in "company culture," or how a group of people likes to operate with one another repeatedly. It's tough for designers to understand a company's culture through interviewing, but interviewers also pick up signals on how you might (or might not) integrate with their culture.

When the differences are around behavior, beliefs, values, and other "cultural" influences, there's not much you can do to improve other than look at how you convey your principles. You can control your ability to communicate how you would align to or add to a company's culture. You can't control whether or not the company's culture would mesh well with you. So if you suspect the rejection was for company culture reasons, best to move on until you can find a better-suited company.

**Consider the competition.**

In many cases, designers are rejected simply because someone else was a better fit for the role (i.e., they had more experience, relevance, or something else). While this can be frustrating, it's important to remember that there will always be someone who is more qualified than you for any given position, skill, experience, etc.

The key is not to let rejection discourage you and instead use it as motivation to keep improving your skills and qualifications so that next time around, you'll be the one who gets hired.

It's ok to feel bad when you get rejected from a job (it's human, after all). If you need to take time away from interviewing to reflect and be with your feelings, know it's ok to do so! As long as you remember that rejection is rarely (if ever) about you as a person. You're capable of great things, learning and improving, and creating influence and impact where you land. So if you've been rejected, keep searching.

**What to do next**

**If you've been rejected from a job after submitting your application, or if you've been rejected after an initial conversation:**

- Ensure you've done enough research into the types of roles and companies you are applying to before applying again.
- Build a consistent and homogeneous set of materials for presenting yourself. Include in your résumé and digital portfolio the same title and language or phrases you see in job posts.
- Ask for community feedback on your résumé and digital portfolio.
- Invest in learning how to better communicate and sell yourself while building your interviewing confidence.
- Check that your career goals are aligned with the types of jobs you're seeking. If you feel stuck, ask for community perspectives on your past experience or education and the types of jobs you're applying to or finding interesting.

**If you've been rejected after multiple conversations with a company:**

- Make sure you understand what interviewers are looking for before you go into an interview. Problem solving exercises, user research exercises, take home assignments, and exploratory interviews are the most common types of interviews you'll need to be prepared for.

- Create a portfolio presentation that aligns your strengths with the types of jobs you apply to, and ensure your presentation is interesting and clear.
- Find a close peer or partner who can practice interviewing with you.

# SIX
# WHERE TO GO FROM HERE

If you've read most or all of the content in this guide, you should now clearly understand the recruiting processes, practices, and conventions designers face today. More importantly: you should have confidence in your ability to move your career forward, whatever that means for you at this point.

If you set a goal for this guide, take a minute to reflect on the outcome of your exploration. Did you achieve what you set out to—why or why not? What did you uncover that was most surprising to you? What felt particularly informative, and what did you struggle with as you read?

Recruiting is a complicated process because it deals with no absolutes. People are complex and companies, consisting of many different people, are more so. Identifying people who can join a team and perform at their best is hard and only sometimes fruitful. Similarly, interviewing can be time-consuming and mentally as well as physically exhausting. But it's also an incredible opportunity to learn about yourself and others, explore and see how others work, reflect on what matters most to you and your career, and contemplate your experience.

The trick to successful interviewing—regardless of whether or not you get the job you're seeking—is to be mindful and curious more than anxious and desperate.

Putting in the work to reflect on your values and past experiences can help create a coherent and consistent story about yourself. In turn, the story you tell yourself and others as part of interviewing will better equip you to identify job opportunities that align with your skills and abilities. And that can lead to better conversations with interviewers.

What should you do next with the information you now have? Put it into action, share it with someone you think could use it, and continue investing in yourself by sharing your personal career story with others. Of all the interviewing lessons I have learned over my career, one of the most impactful has been the importance of being open and vulnerable. When we share our career stories with others in any form, we give ourselves a chance to tune our beliefs about ourselves to reality. And what we find in those stories is often a shining light of skill, ability, and growth. When we hear others' careers stories, it's like looking into a mirror that shows us our characteristics and paths—often ones we lose track of in the muck of our day-to-day responsibilities.

Whether you recognize it or not, your career is a story, and interviewing is ultimately a storytelling process. When you show up with a solid story, others will pay attention and find a connection.

Define your story, find ways to share it with others, and your career ambitions or goals will follow.

# ABOUT TANNER CHRISTENSEN

Tanner Christensen is an experienced, curious, and versatile product designer with more than 20 years of experience designing and building digital products across web and mobile platforms. He resides in California and Illinois with his wife and two dogs.

Previously, Tanner led design at Gem.com, where he built the design function and team from scratch. Before Gem, Tanner was a lead designer of software for autonomous vehicles at Lyft, led the Atlassian mobile systems platform's design, and designed for nearly three billion people at Facebook across both business and consumer products.

Additionally, Tanner defines himself as a creative designer specializing in product strategy, visual, and interaction design. He has considerable experience in design thinking, content strategy, software engineering (web and mobile), accessibility design, design systems, and more.

His work has been quoted and referenced in numerous publications, including The New Yorker, Forbes, Fast Company, The New York Times, The Huffington Post, Lifehacker, Wired, Kottke, Boing Boing, and American Express OPEN Forum.

In 2015 Tanner's first book was published—The Creativity Challenge: Design, Experiment, Test, Innovate, Build, Create, Inspire, and Unleash Your Genius.

To learn more about Tanner or his work, visit tannerc.com.

Made in the USA
Las Vegas, NV
29 August 2024

94576571R00125